How We Want to Live

NARRATIVES ON PROGRESS

EDITED BY

SUSAN RICHARDS SHREVE AND **PORTER SHREVE**

INTRODUCTION BY JAMES RESTON, JR.

BEACON PRESS

BOSTON

BEACON PRESS
25 Beacon Street
Boston, Massachusetts 02108-2892
www.beacon.org

BEACON PRESS BOOKS
are published under the auspices of
the Unitarian Universalist Association of Congregations.

03 02 01 00 99 98   8 7 6 5 4 3 2 1

This book is printed on recycled acid-free paper that contains at least 20 percent
postconsumer waste and meets the uncoated paper ANSI/NISO specifications for
permanence as revised in 1992.

Text design by Elizabeth Elsas
Composition by Wilsted & Taylor Publishing Services

Library of Congress Cataloging-in-Publication Data
How we want to live : narratives on progress / edited by Susan
    Richards Shreve and Porter Shreve ; introduction by James Reston,
    Jr.
        p.   cm.
    ISBN 0-8070-4510-1 (cloth)
    1. Progress.   2. Civilization, Modern.   3. Technology and
civilization.   4. Quality of life.   5. Conduct of life.   I. Shreve,
Susan Richards.   II. Shreve, Porter.
    HM101.H758   1998
    303.44—dc21   98-14292

CONTENTS

CONTENTS

PREFACE

I was just out of college on my first trip to Europe, a member of the generation of students for whom *relativity* was a sacred word. In Florence, walking along a winding street towards the Duomo, I rounded a corner and there on the Bapistry were Lorenzo Ghiberti's bronze doors—The Gates of Paradise. I had memorized these doors in my introductory art history class, examined their projection on the screen in the front of the lecture hall, understood their history, studied each small figure, knew the details. Though I knew of course that they were doors, I had not imagined them as actual ones, utilitarian, on a building, surviving centuries. For a moment, relativity lost its value, the years of student defenses slipped away and I was struck by the grandness of human imagination, its capacity to fix in place a moment in history, its permanence.

How We Want to Live: Narratives on Progress is the second book in a series of original essays in which narrative writers have been asked to address a concept, a grand idea, one which has particular resonance in our culture. The first of these collections, *Outside the Law: Narratives on Justice in America,* published by Beacon Press in 1997, began with conversations around our dinner table among generations of children and grown children and parents, spanning in age much of the century.

What has happened, we wondered, to our understanding of ideas like justice or progress or religion in a century in which so much has changed? The conversations turned into a book when we thought of asking narrative writers to consider justice—storytellers whose particular gift of imagination and empathy can capture the heart of an idea like justice, give it life, and move us to understanding.

Of course progress should be the subject of this second collection of essays. Or so we thought, imagining in many of the pieces we would receive a kind of optimism, a celebration of our technological age. After all, progress defines how we think of ourselves as Americans, the sense we had growing up that our lives are getting better and better, that the future is brighter than the past.

We invited writers for whom progress has been a subject of interest, expecting some, like the naturalist Bill McKibben or Annie Dillard, to conclude that the laws of nature are holy laws and human progress is sometimes in the way of or incidental to them. We knew that Kirkpatrick Sale's work questions the value of progress. But there were many from whom we expected a different point of view, like the novelist Alan Lightman who is also a physicist; or the novelist, playwright, and social critic Ishmael Reed, who has changed the way we understand the multiplicity of our culture; or John Barth, whose fiction deconstructs language and whose work has altered the way we look at narrative. Instead, as you will see, progress in these essays is ultimately personal, even when it becomes public. Progress is an individual response to the world in which we live, not a concept and not a construct.

The title *How We Want to Live* recognizes the personal in these essays, recognizes that the technological advances with which we associate progress in the twentieth century have added to our lives and have, as well, taken away from them. We are not entirely in control of what technology has wrought, any more than we are in control of earthquakes or tornadoes or long glorious days of sunshine. But we do have choices. We can make a selection for our own lives, and it is those choices which this collection addresses.

When my children were small, I was driving with a car full of little boys, and one of them asked what kind of car I was driving. My younger son, sitting next to me in the front seat, turned to his friend.

"Don't ask my mother that," he said, sadly. "She thinks we're traveling in a horse and buggy."

Perhaps I could have imagined a horse and buggy as he said, but I wouldn't want to have one. A buggy is too slow and I couldn't handle the horse. Nevertheless what these essays and stories ask you to do is consider the alternatives, to know what you can handle, to make a decision to live with integrity, so that the story of a life, perhaps more than at any time in our history, can be made by you.

—SUSAN RICHARDS SHREVE

JAMES RESTON, JR.

Introduction

Not long ago, at a small specialized hospital outside Front Royal, Virginia, I was invited to witness a rare procedure on the frontier of medicine. The experience seems to me to bring the question of progress into high relief. The operation that day took place in the brave new world of fertility and reproduction, and thus, my briefing began in the laboratory. There, a postdoctoral specialist from Australia treated me to a short lecture on the new science of cryobiology, on the fundamentals of ovulation, on the procedures for calibrating sperm count, and on past and present methods of cell culture. Then, as a special treat, she prepared a few slides for me, taking droplets from her tray of vials, dimming the light, and directing me toward a fluorescent microscope. In an incredible fish pond of virile tadpoles, the live and dead cells of the anonymous male donor had been stained with different colors. Therefore, it was possible to determine how many active sperm cells would be inserted in the patient's womb a few minutes later. The numbers of these impressive little critters ran into the tens of thousands, but only one, well placed, was enough for a score. It would not be as easy as it appeared.

Then came the announcement. The patient (who, for obvious privacy reasons, I will call Clarice Williams) had been safely put to sleep and all was ready. Outside the operating room, the doctor in charge of the procedure greeted me warmly, for he was glad to speak to an outsider about this new and revolutionary work. Quickly, he realized that my appreciation of medical nomenclature was virtually nil, and so he stuck an ultrasound image of Clarice's ovary in front of me. This was all a bit elemental for me, as he explained how the insertion of the sperm cells would proceed, what the chances of success might be, and what the implications were for the long-range, worldwide uses of these techniques into the next century and the next millennium. With great pride he announced that in the previous year his team had achieved five successful pregnancies.

In the simple operating suite, more than a dozen experts crowded around the operating table. As I pressed against a back wall, feeling like an interloper at this almost sacred moment, my host whispered her introductions of who each person was and what his or her role was in the procedure. The normal complement of high-tech medical machines was ready at hand, beeping and flashing, especially the pulse oximeter which monitored Ms. Williams' pulse and heart rate as well as her blood pressure. A tube protruded from the vicinity of the patient's leg, the intravenous drip that carried a saline solution and whose function was to ensure a quick recovery in the post-operative phase. The anesthesiologist—the real point man here, since it was his job to make sure that all life signs were strong and stable—had come from Children's Hospital in Washington. He sat grim faced by the patient's head, mopping her brow and watching the various monitors keenly.

I was impressed and touched. This was remarkable work: laudable in every way; impossible, for a number of reasons, only a few years ago; and replete with implications for the next century. And so I stepped back, restraining my curiosity and my loquaciousness, and let them get on with it.

I suppose I should mention that Clarice Williams is a scimitar-horned oryx, and therefore, she has an exotic background. Her roots are in a lost tribe of African antelopes that has suffered virtual genocide in the past century and now exists only on reservations like this high-fenced preserve in the hills above Front Royal. Only about 1200 of her fellow creatures survive. The purpose of the effort is to increase the number of this endangered species, along with such other exotics like the black-footed ferret, ideally to the point where they can be re-introduced into the African wild.

The only problem is that there is virtually no African wild left into which Clarice's brood might be introduced. Even if there were, in a perfect place, say, like the highlands of Tunisia, there are no administrators or specialists there to manage and nurture the herd, much less to protect it from poachers and other hazards of man's inexorable encroachment.

And so here in this magnificent, vulnerable beast, with its banded, curved, sadly obsolete horns pressing against its fur-lined backbone, was the dilemma of progress incarnate. The amazing techniques of modern medicine are harnessed to a poignant lost cause: to preserve exotic animals from extinction even though there really is no place for them anymore on the man-wasted earth. Toward what purpose? Only to satisfy the needs of the world's zoos, it seems, to ensure that more children around the world might be able to gawk at one of these imprisoned throwbacks behind bars, and more adults might ponder with sadness the question of how diverse and wondrous the biology of the world once was.

Outside the operating room the doctor pronounced his ultimate irony. The advances in human fertility: test tube babies, in vitro fertilization, and the ability to recover and preserve human embryos were paying great dividends for their work with endangered species. "Come back in eleven months," the doctor called after me as I was leaving, "and we'll let you know if we were successful today." I wished him good luck.

In this collection of essays, seventeen writers ponder the puzzle of progress, that devilish "archetypal trope," as Rebecca Walker calls it. They hold varying opinions about the origins of the concept. In the Renaissance. In Christian theology. In Puritan England. Perhaps in the Depression. And they differ about how progress should be defined. Human happiness. Greater comfort. Faster speed in transportation and communication. Reduction in human suffering. Dazzling technology. Longer life span.

Measuring such things is difficult, partly because there seems to

be no objective standard. "More people inhabit the planet with pleasure than ever before," Nicholas Delbanco asserts. "The weight of
progress overwhelms." Not everyone agrees. To certify progress
seems to be a matter of what one passionately values . . . and what one
passionately despises. How do we balance any one of these positive
abstractions against regression? Against poverty, AIDS, the scourge
of drugs, environmental disaster, the impoverishment of family life?
In his essay "Five Facets of a Myth," for example, Kirkpatrick Sale
generalizes from my afternoon in the hills of Front Royal: 500,000
species have been lost to our world in the past century alone. This is
a shocking, but also controversial statistic. My friends in Front Royal
are more conservative. They hold to a lower number: the world only
loses 1500 species every year.

If that is backward motion, so what? How important is it anyway?
Who cares? Why not accent the positive? It is sad . . . but how sad
really when we capture "virtually" the same thing electronically?
Sale persists in his statistics that have been laid upon the altar of progress: 56 million acres of forestland are being denuded every year. Desertification threatens eight billion acres of land worldwide. All seventeen of the world's major fisheries are in decline. The figures are
unforgiving.

Dark considerations of a different sort preoccupy other writers.
Ishmael Reed, not generally known as an environmentalist, refers to
the mess that we have made of our planet in the name of progress.
Fish with sores and heroin addicts in the suburbs strike him as apt
symbols. Pearl Abraham, by contrast, laments the fractured tradition of the Jewish extended family speaking Yiddish in America, at
the same time as she celebrates the greater sense of security in America's diaspora. From the Asian American perspective Shawn Wong
worries about his own sense of rootlessness (and that of other Asian
Americans) as a piece of "hollow bamboo." Janna Malamud Smith
mourns the loss of her youthful passions about a better world, forged
in the civil rights and Vietnam eras and asks the poignant but highly
relevant question: How do you make dreams of progress for people
who have arrived? Noelle Oxenhandler picks up on that theme and
suggests that progress is better understood against a backdrop of

scarcity or deprivation or oppression. In the incredible speed of modern transportation and communication she mourns the loss of the "intermediate zone," that time for reflection that previous generations had as they were trying to get somewhere or reach someone far away. All writers of narrative know the importance of daydreaming.

Some of these writers are less interested in social or global progress. Perhaps that is the storyteller's bent. Only personal progress is worth pondering, some believe, as if the world is too complicated to balance forward and backward motion, as if the human race is too mixed up between the forces of good and evil, pleasure and pain, liberty and oppression to make a judgment, as if only ironies are important. Bruce Duffy, for example, wears his ambivalence openly: "I speak out of both sides of my mouth," he confesses with admirable honesty, "enjoying the fruits of technological and material progress, even as I high-mindedly shake my head at what it has wrought." Alan Cheuse gets it straight from his students: "Personal progress, that's all we have left," he is told bluntly. And Porter Shreve, a grudging member of the first generation to grow up on computers, fears the loss of genuine community, of personal connection, in the "made by you" digital age.

Both Bill McKibben and Alan Lightman reject the separation between personal and collective progress. "My work in environmental issues has made me wary of completely private solutions," McKibben writes. "Aren't we ethically impelled to try and imagine ways that such private solutions might turn into public and widespread progress?" It is an old debate. Lightman, in turn, sees today's technology overload as both a national and personal malaise.

In all this earnest head-scratching lies the value of this collection. The idea of progress has been left too long to the sociologists and their dry data and jargon-filled tracts, or to the politicians and their platitudes. Let's put the problem in real terms. Let's look for answers in the ordinary, concrete situation, rather than in glorious abstractions and in glittering generalities.

To ask narrative writers to address so elusive a subject as progress is to get several things: a new slant, rooted in humanity, replete with earthy storytelling, profound sincerity, the courage to deal with the problem emotionally, the certainty of diverse opinions. These writers are drawn to drama and allusion, to symbol and to irony. They are capable of handling contradiction. And so at times you will be wondering what the writer is getting at, and how it relates to the subject.

Be patient. That's the fun of the collection. A lot of good and pertinent stories are told here. To think about progress may be to reflect, as the poet Susan Wood does, on your years of psychoanalysis, concluding, "What I do know is the truth of uncertainty. To believe otherwise is to believe in the myth of the straight line, the myth of progress." Or to consider the benefits of e-mail, like the linguist Deborah Tannen, who compares her life of technological connectedness to the life of her father, a Polish immigrant, separated from his past, disconnected from nearly all of his family, except in memory. Or to believe, as John Barth suggests in his hilarious story involving a squished cat and a sexy Good Samaritan that, as the past relates to the future, what goes around comes around.

Because in fiction writers draw so heavily on their own experience, our contributors look to touchstones, those vibrant, emotional, defining moments in their lives that freight their attitude toward themselves or toward their world. For ultimately the question of progress relates to an attitude of hope or of pessimism. When he thinks about American progress, the space shots of his youth come to Bruce Duffy's mind as beacons, even as he knows that the glories of the lunar landings were a response to Sputnik and Yury Gagarin. The lesson: progress can come from the competition of adversaries. Other events torment Janna Malamud Smith: the assassination of the Kennedys and Martin Luther King, Jr., of My Lai, the Chicago Convention, the napalmed girl, and the Cambodian invasion. Together and alone, without counterpoint, those events put us back in Machiavelli's Italy. To Alan Cheuse's outspoken students the notion of progress exploded in the New Mexico desert with the detonation of the first atomic bomb. After that, only personal progress mattered. And Annie Dillard carries this point one step further: she notes how we have become emotionally and psychologically numbed to the huge disasters of our time, like the 1991 flood in Bangladesh which killed 138,000 people in one day. In the grip of such mathematical magnitudes, she wonders how we can recapture our sense of tragedy at the loss of a single life.

This collection, therefore, does what any good collection of essays should do. While it entertains and enlightens, it also presents a challenge: it encourages you to choose your own touchstones. Then you must weight them with significance: whose footstep is more important to you, Neil Armstrong's or William Calley's? Which explosion colors your attitude more: Hiroshima or Cape Canaveral? If these questions are too abstract, maybe there's a squished cat and a Good Samaritan in your life.

Be careful. Your choices may say more about you than they do about your world.

It seems only fair to accept the challenge. My touchstones?

On the playing fields of Chapel Hill I look up to the contrails of jets speeding toward Florida during the Cuban Missile Crisis, and I know that we will all die in a few days. (The worst part of it seems that in these preliberation days, we are going to die as virgins.) But the world pulled back from nuclear apocalypse then, and it has pulled way back from the brink of nuclear war between superpowers now. That is progress.

At the Watts Motel, the last segregated public accommodation in town, we lie limp and singing on the lawn next to the roadway until Mrs. Watts, near 300 pounds, storms out, squats over my friend and our leader, John Dunn, and urinates on him. But the South has rid itself of legal segregation, and that is progress.

Ron Ray, my GI buddy, refuses our harebrained commander's order to play on the unit's softball team in Hawaii, volunteers for Vietnam in a huff, and is killed in Hue during the Tet Offensive. But America is more sensitive now toward pointless death and, I trust, will never again have another war like Vietnam. That is certainly progress.

My first book, my first wife, my first child: these were achievements, a kind of progress. But would there be more? Yes, more books, more children, only one wife.

After my first child is born, I stand in a plowed field of Jonestown, two weeks after the event, amid discarded potties and baby bottles: that represented a kind of progress, neutral anyway, because I went crazy only for a week or so and later recovered my sanity.

And now we wait for a transplant for our third child. Waiting is hard, yes, and it is true that waiting is longer since the level of generosity in the population is less. But we also know that thirty years ago, Hillary would have been long since dead. Science and freedom sometimes go together, as Alan Cheuse points out. In Hillary's case, science means freedom from death. But there is a price. In her essay Annie Dillard asks an excruciating question, far more excruciating than perhaps she knows when the answer is not abstract but concrete. "If sanctioning the death of strangers could save my daughter's life, would I do it? Probably." To receive the gift of a human organ usually involves the death of a stranger. To think about that is almost unbearable for the recipient. So progress in the real world is rarely a pristine question of cold mathematical calculation.

After considering these essays, pondering the question from the long view and from the vantage point of this moment, from the global to the personal, I tilt on the side of progress. It is in my nature, to be sure. But I stand with Susan Wood: perhaps there is no city on the hill, no promised land, no ultimate state of perfection . . . and no inevitable forward motion. And at the same time, I will have to think further about the assertion of Rebecca Walker's accomplished friend: the basic ratio of good to evil always stays the same no matter what.

PEARL ABRAHAM

Lost Souls

Our home was open to people from every Jewish denomination, especially the down-and-out who were in some kind of trouble; "the lost souls," my father called them. A frequent and not untypical Friday night dinner guest was a young man who was a compulsive gambler and whose wife finally left him when she discovered on the first day of Hanukah that he'd sold their silver menorah.

"The poor woman had to use potatoes to hold the candles," my father said, holding up her misfortune as a lesson to us: This is what happens to those who veer away from the true path; this is what goes on in the modern world.

In our world, which included the day-to-day management of a small congregation, it was not unusual to wake up in the morning to the sounds of our father rehearsing the portions of the Torah to be read in the synagogue that week. Before holidays, he would practice certain prayer tunes, especially those he'd bungled the year before. Orthodox services are always a capella. There is no musical accompaniment to help the cantor, unlike the services of Reform temples where organs are used.

Like a church, my father would say. Those Reformists have turned the synagogue into a church.

But what about all the modern Jews (we used the word *moderene* which included modern Orthodox, Conservative, and Reform Jews, pretty much everyone who was not Hasidic) who are not gamblers and thieves? They look down on us. Our own great-uncle, the Conservative rabbi from Long Island, says Hasidic women are mere baby machines.

No one looks down on us, my father said. They want to be like us. And our uncle is unfortunately a deluded man who will come knocking at our door one day.

This was also the answer he gave when we were just off the boat and still wearing the ankle-high, white-polished shoes which attracted so much negative attention at school. Everyone else wore sensible Buster Browns. Buster Browns were what we wanted, but we wouldn't get them until we outgrew the shoes we had. That first year in America is marked by the memory that my feet stopped growing.

This year, on the eve of the Jewish new year, my sister and I went to services together. We walked two blocks down to the nearby temple renowned for great cantors and large enough to be anonymous. When we arrived the doors were locked and a posted sign directed nonmembers to a 6:30 service at the Christ Scientist Church. (Anticipating a crowd larger than the temple could accommodate, the management rented church space for holiday services.) It was already 6:35 and we hurried, uncertain of the exact location of this neighboring church. On arrival there was already a line of nonmembers waiting, and we weren't the last ones; taxi cabs pulled up to the curb and others joined us. Would we hear any of the prayers today? Finally the doors opened; we walked up three flights and found a good place from which to hear and see.

An organ accompanied the choir; the song was not a prayer familiar to me or my sister. Two young men who seemed to be leading the service spoke of what the new year signifies. They stood facing one another and speaking slowly, voices modulated, as if conducting a dialogue. I don't know what they said; my attention was diverted by the staged aspect of the conversation. Then a woman was helped up to the platform and using a microphone proceeded to sing what sounded like an old lullaby.

My sister looked at me. Was this a Rosh Hashana service?

We left fifteen minutes later, without having heard any of our old favorites. What happened to the sobering prayer about who will live and who will die? What about the plaintive "Our Father / Our King / We sinned before you"? My sister started the chant, I joined her, and we walked home humming the prayers, which in another city our father and brothers might have been chanting at the same time.

Over the years friends have recommended various temples and rabbis. At the top of everyone's list are those with a special spiritual touch, but it is this touch that bothers me, this pitch toward the spiritual and away from the plain-spoken warnings, predictions, even threats that turn the Rosh Hashana service I know into something like a refined version of the sit-ins of the seventies.

The facts: I look and am cut of the same cloth as the other non-members in that crowd. I too might have arrived in a taxi; I too went home and, with the exception of the ritual dipping of fruit into honey, spent the evening in much the same way I spend other evenings.

More facts: Despite my objections to the Reform service, I do not have plans to attend an Orthodox one on Yom Kippur. I am not an Orthodox Jew. Nor am I a Reform or Conservative Jew.

My father believes that the versions of Judaism practiced by Reform and Conservative congregations are not Jewish at all, but some other religion, which makes walking into a Reform temple as bad as walking into a church. For an Orthodox Jew that's a sin. That services were in fact held at the Christ Scientist Church would only confirm his argument.

Ten years ago, I would not have attended any service. Fifteen years ago, in an act of defiance, my sister and I spent a Yom Kippur day in bed, reading and watching television, waiting for the day to pass. (Although we weren't in the synagogue, we were fasting.) Is this year's yearning for traditional services a sign of progress or regression? In one's fearless teens and twenties, judgments are harsh and pure. With life experience comes greater understanding and empathy; with age comes nostalgia; a fuller, rounder view of the world is achieved, but there is some weakness at the heart of it all.

In my teens, I stopped speaking Yiddish outside the confines of home. This wasn't an intentional act, just a matter of circumstances. We spoke English in school and therefore with friends; home was the only other universe. A positive side effect was that my English improved. A negative: My Yiddish vocabulary remained at pre–high school levels and I lost fluency in the language.

In the family lexicon of bloopers are literal translations from English to Yiddish and vice versa which inevitably come up at the end of family gatherings. No matter how frequent or repetitive, these recountings continue to produce much laughter (tears in my father's eyes) and delayed good-byes.

Sometime in my twenties I stopped dreaming in Yiddish, and although this was an internal and involuntary change, to family members and myself there seemed to be an external difference.

I was in college at the time, studying English literature. I did not join the campus Hillel group nor did I attend Jewish-oriented events. In fact, I didn't tell people that I'd grown up in a Hasidic home. It wasn't a secret, merely a fact about me that seemed to have no relevance to my life in the modern world. At the same time, I found myself unable to translate details of my daily existence to my parents; I couldn't find the Yiddish words that would express anxieties about career (this was the eighties), identity, or success. Which meant that there was no one who knew me entirely; I was painfully a stranger everywhere.

Over the years people have tried their Yiddish on me, but with their limited knowledge of the language and our differing dialects, there was always a distance between us and I barely responded. Not that I didn't encounter various Yiddish dialects growing up. Among my siblings it is still common today to use a Polish Yiddish when addressing our mother and a Hungarian version with our father. At the various grade schools I attended other dialects were spoken and I became a kind of chameleon of the Yiddish language, which would lead one to suppose that I could speak it with anyone from anywhere.

It came as a surprise, therefore, when on tour with my first novel in Germany, a Jewish interviewer addressing me in Yiddish brought a red flush to my face and neck. Attempting to fall in with his accent and not fully succeeding, I managed a mumbled Yiddish reply and embarrassed myself in the process. I was out of practice. But there was something else that made me uncomfortable. He suggested that we conduct the entire interview in Yiddish and I declined, knowing that I would not have the necessary vocabulary with which to discuss literature or my novel; at best, it would have been a struggle.

Given that, in the novel under discussion, I had worked hard to evoke in my characters' English the cadences of Yiddish, my difficulty with the language seemed strange. And the shame I felt over the whole episode puzzled me.

I called my sister from Germany and as usual in our conversations, we said certain Yiddish expressions in Yiddish because they don't translate well and because there is for us always a certain humor and satisfaction in pulling out the right expression for a given moment. I attempted fuller Yiddish sentences and found myself pretty much at home with the language. The difficulty: Yiddish had become for me a language of intimacy; I could speak it comfortably only with members of my family.

In retrospect, it seems that some of the discomfort may have had to do with the fact that I was in Germany speaking Yiddish, and that the interview was being filmed for television. Conducted in Yiddish, the interview would become a performance. It is probably for similar reasons that I am unwilling to respond when someone asks me to say something in Yiddish.

One of the consequences of the Zionist movement's popularity was that Yiddish, the language of European Jews, was more or less lost. As a stepchild of lower German, the argument went, Yiddish isn't a language the Jews ought to bring to their new country; Hebrew, on the other hand, has always been the true and pure Semitic language; the Bible, after all, is written in it. The Reform and Conservative movements in America took their cues from the Zionists and started teaching Hebrew. Remaining speakers of Yiddish were for the most part refugees from Nazi Europe: older people and also the Hasidim of Eastern Europe. Today the older people are dying (or no longer alive) which is why Yiddish is said to be a dead language. Among Hasidim in New York, however, it is alive and growing. Just as there once were Polish, Hungarian, Russian, and other dialects of Yiddish, in the hands of the Hasidim, the language is showing American influences; Yinglish, some call it.

But I attended a school that wasn't Hasidic; many of my teachers had never heard Yiddish spoken. Hebrew texts studied in classrooms were translated into English; school exams and papers were written in Hebrew or English. I was twelve the last time I wrote anything significant in that language and it was a response to a sweetly innocent love letter from my younger brother; we were both away at camp, both lonely; and although our campgrounds were less than twenty miles apart, we didn't see one another all summer.

When I started writing, I found that the characters I wanted to bring to the page were Yiddish speakers. These were the people who interested me. Yiddish was the language I wanted to evoke. After all those years of learning that Hebrew is valued above Yiddish, my loyalties had not changed. Some mornings at my desk, a Yiddish word or phrase would be in my head and for the rest of that day, everything I wrote seemed influenced by that phrase.

With the prevailing inclination to celebrate ethnicity, modern American Jews, whose sense of security in this country has deepened, are showing renewed interest in Hasidim. No longer do I hear about the long black coats that attract too much attention. Nor do I hear about Hasidic ignorance. In fact, the second and third generations of American Jews have been looking toward their traditional heritage for patterns on which to model their lives.

I stand at an odd remove from these fluctuations in favor. After tolerating, even assimilating the criticisms of Hasidim, after accepting then rejecting modern judgments, I read about recent shifts in attitude with skepticism along with some stronger feelings.

*   *   *

A year ago, the phone rang and after twenty years of no contact, my great-uncle was on the phone requesting (demanding?) a visit. Several months and several cancellations later, my sister and I had dinner with him and his wife on a Friday night. They met us at the door and I had a difficult time reconciling my child's view of these seemingly significant and somehow powerful people with the aged, needy, and so much shorter than I remembered husband and wife.

My uncle complained. How is it, he wanted to know, that with so many nieces and nephews, he had no visitors, no table full of guests at which to conduct a Friday night meal?

What about your children and grandchildren? I asked.

They're busy, he said.

His daughter does medical research at a prestigious university hospital and his son, who has two children, works in computers.

We did see our grandchildren this summer, my uncle said. They live in Massachusetts which is far away.

What he misses, his wife explained, are the large families of his youth, people who are at home more and whom you could visit on Shabbat.

My sister and I looked at one another. Our father's prediction had come true.

Of course we won't tell him.

JOHN BARTH

Dead Cat, Floating Boy

If I weren't an already happily married man, it might have been what screenwriters call a Cute Meet: end of a spring afternoon in Baltimore; rush-hour traffic exiting the city on the arterial that ran past our house; my wife off doing family errands while I scratch out yet another sentence or two before happy hour; doorbell-chime interruption of—perhaps by?—the muse. I cap my pen ungrudgingly (longish workday, story stuck), and from the pitch of the bell decide en route downstairs from my worktable that the ringer is at our seldom-used street-facing door. Ignoring its peephole out of trusting country habit, I duly undo that portal's city bolts and chains, et voila: a tall, slender, uncommonly handsome early-thirtyish woman in white sweatshirt, black leotard, and considerable distress. Dark hair drawn back in short ponytail; New-Age-looking headband of some sort; fine high cheekbones (was anyone ever described as having *low* cheekbones?); tears welling in her I-forget-what-color eyes behind wire-rimmed specs.

Can I help her?

She doesn't know. Do I own a black-and-white cat?

Afraid not.

Maybe one of my neighbors does?

Could be . . . ?

The car just in front of hers, she explains, just struck just such a cat just up the street and just kept right on going. She stopped and tried to help; fears the poor thing's hurt really badly; wondered if it belongs to one of these houses; decided she'd try to get help even though she's illegally parked and backing up traffic and running late for her yoga class out in Towson. Nobody home next door, so here she is. Excuse her sniffles (she removes her glasses and dabs her eyes with a sweatshirt sleeve); she just recently lost her own cat to just such a hit-and-runner.

Let's have a look.

The arterial is indeed clogged, its two outbound lanes squeezing into one to pass her hazard-blinking gray Honda. Impatient commuters honk as she leads me across the front lawn toward a white bundle on the curbside of the Episcopal church, two doors up. Oh be quiet! she calls in their general direction: You're not dying!

To her shapely back I observe Not at the same rate, anyhow, and she gives me an over-the-shoulder smile. I'm twice her age. So what? And anyhow, so what?

I wrapped the poor thing in a towel, she says as we reach it; it's all I could think to do. Her voice is a hormoned contralto, stirring even in distress. I know you're not supposed to move them, but I couldn't just leave it in the street, you know?

Let's have a look. As if I'm a veterinarian paramedic instead of a stalled storyteller, I hunker with her over the victim and peel back the towel. Big black-bodied, white-nosed/-bibbed/-forepawed tom, sleek of coat, well fed, unsquished—indeed unmarked, on the upside anyhow, although there's a spot of blood on the towel under his terminally snarled mouth. Doornail dead.

What do you think? she asks tautly. Our faces are a foot apart. Fine estrogenic Mediterranean-looking skin over those aforenoted cheekbones.

Kaput, I'm afraid. I point to the bloodstain. Internal bleeding.

She makes a tight-throat sound, strokes the glossy fur. One of the bottlenecked commuters is actually pounding the outside of his car door through the open window. *Stop that!* she all but hisses himward. Like a television doctor, I draw her towel back over the deceased. Then stand. Neither a pet lover nor a pet hater, I find myself unmoved by the anonymous animal's demise except in the most general tisk-tisk way. I rather admire Ms. Leotard's more emotional response; she's still hunkered, reluctant to accept the tomcat's death, while I'm coldheartedly though warmbloodedly appraising her excellent neck and shoulders, lithe-muscled legs and compact butt, imagining them-all in the Lotus position, for example. Back when my children were children there were important cats and dogs—but that was decades ago, in another life.

Now she stands, too. The backed-up traffic extends by this time all the way to the stoplight down the block. I imagine a TV news camera shooting the scene artsily from pavement level: dead cat on curb, framed by car bumpers; mourners standing tall, heads bent, the woman's outfit nicely echoing the deceased's; church spire in background, pointing to Cat Heaven.

May she use my phone to call the animal disposal people?

I find momentarily piquant the thought of her in my house, using my telephone, and then loyally reprove myself: It's *our* house, *our* telephone, *our* monogamously happy life. Better get on to your yoga class, I advise her, before the cops impound your car. I'll pop the poor guy into a garbage bag and put him out with my trash.

She gives me a full-faced look of lovely concern. Won't he get yucky? When's your pick-up date?

Not to worry; I'll take care of it. I even retrieve her blood-spotted towel. Here you go, now.

She smiles, takes the towel, touches my forearm lightly with her other long-fingered hand, looks wonderfully into my eyes with her, oh, forget-me-not-colored ones, and thanks me *so* much.

Not a problem. Have a good life.

So wide and moist a smile. You too!

When I return with a plastic garbage bag the gray Honda is gone, and traffic on the arterial has resumed its normal rush-hour flow. The limp cat corpse, hoisted by the tail for headfirst bagging, is surprisingly heavy. Uncertain of city regulations in the matter, I incorporate the bundle into a larger bag half full of leaves and weeds and put the whole into a tightly lidded trash can at the alley end of our driveway, trusting that it won't stink by pick-up time, two days hence.

Over wine and hors d'oeuvres a short while later on our backyard porch, I retail to my homecome mate an edited version of the little incident. Cute Meet, we agree, and toast our own of so long past.

I hope and trust that she *has* had, is having as I write this, a good life, that emotionally and physically endowed young woman. The first of three sequels to our encounter is a note from her in the mail shortly thereafter—on garbage collection day, in fact, when the remains of our path-crossing occasion passed without incident into the municipal trash-stream. Addressed to *Good Samaritan* (with the same presence of mind that had concerned her regarding "our" cat's potential yuckiness, Ms. Leotard had either made mental note of my street address or—intriguing thought—had returned to the scene postyogaly to register it, perhaps to verify as well that I had done my promised job), it read only *Thank you, kind sir,* and, parenthesized under illegible initials, (*the cat lady*). No name or return address; I liked that. *End of Story,* it declared in effect, as if she had sensed . . . and, like me, had dismissed. . . .

The stuck story that this nonadventure relieved me from was meant to have been inspired by a season-old item in the daily newspaper of the southwest Florida city where my wife and I had spent the winter prior to this dead-cat Baltimore spring. In mangrove marshes well up the Gulf Coast from our rented condominium, a fat and severely autistic ten-year-old boy had somehow "drifted away" from his parents and siblings at a swimming hole, the article reported, into the vast circumambient swamp. Over several following days and nights, while helicopters, air boats, swamp buggies, and foot-slogging rescuers searched in vain, he had floated through the warm, labyrinthine waterways: naked (he seems to have shucked his shorts somewhere along the way), oblivious to snakes and alligators and mosquitoes, buoyed up and insulated from hypothermia by his obesity, entertained by the sight of those overflying machines. Evidently he quenched his thirst as necessary from the freshmarsh water he floated in; no one knows whether and what he ate. On the fourth day he was spotted by a sport fisherman and retrieved—unalarmed and evidently unharmed except for incidental scratches and a bit of sun-

burn—a full fourteen miles from the swimming hole. His parents
had no idea, they declared, how he had managed to drift away unre-
marked, to a distance beyond ready refinding. They had alerted the
authorities, they declared, as soon as they noticed his absence. He
wanted to go back, they declared he declared upon his untrauma-
tized restoration themto, to see the helicopters.

Taylor Touchstone, the boy's name was—cross my heart—and in
the weeks following that newspaper account the image of him adrift
among the mangroves like a bloated infant Moses among the cattails
became a touchstone indeed to my imagination: a *floating* touchstone, like the lad himself. As now in the matter of The Dead Cat, I
made notebook entries on The Floating Boy, whose serene misad-
venture spoke to me in a way I recognized. In addition to Moses (set
adrift to escape Pharaoh's massacre of the Hebrew firstborn, then
found and retrieved by his would-be killer's maiden daughter) I
noted other mythic heroes floated off or otherwise rescued in early
childhood from vengeful or fearful authority: baby Perseus snugged
in his sea chest, baby Oedipus plucked from hillside exposure, the
Yavapai-Apache prophet's baby daughter floated off in her cotton-
wood canoe—the list is long. More generally, I noted other voyag-
ers from domesticity into dreamish irreality and back—Odysseus,
Sinbad (the list is even longer)—and floaters into radical metamor-
phosis: sperm and ova, fetuses in the Amniotic Sea—all of us, come
to that, floating through our life stories like unread messages in bottles or galaxies in the void, and into dream-country every mortal
night. *Ukiyo-e,* I made note of: the ephemeral "floating world" of
Japanese painting—and, by association, those as-if-magical Japanese Crackerjack favors of my pre-World-War-II boyhood: tightly
folded little paper somethings that one dropped into a glass of water
and waited for the slow exfoliation of into intricate flowers or
brightly colored castles.

Just so (I noted), like seeds at sea, do art's gametes float in the fancies of those whose calling it is to fertilize and deliver them. Some
sprout/bloom/fruit with the celerity of time-lapse nature films; others eddy like that messaged bottle tossed experimentally into the Pacific by (Japanese) students in August 1985 and found ten years later

on a beach north of Honolulu, the Togane High School Earth Science Club members who launched it having long since graduated and set out upon their own life-voyages. And some, to be sure, remain forever flotsam, embryos no longer gestating in the muse's womb but pickled in the formaldehyde of fruitless notes.

So was it with this suspended floating-touchstone tale, displaced now by the dead-cat interlude with its mild but not insignificant erotic aura (if the doorbell ringer had been male or unattractive, I trust I would have performed the same neighborly service, but my imagination would have been unengaged). "The cat came back," went a song from my small-town childhood; likewise the above-told cat encounter:

> . . . the very next day,
> The cat came back like he'd never been away.

Indeed, the species' homing abilities are so acute that they can be notoriously difficult to ditch; thus (together with their knack for literally landing on their feet) the folk proposition that they have "nine lives." In an afore-alluded-to earlier life-chapter of my own, when I was about that comely cat-woman's age, my then spouse and I prepared to make our maiden expedition to Europe on the occasion of my first sabbatical leave from university teaching. We would pick up a Volkswagen Microbus in Le Havre at autumn's end, camp our way therein down to the Mediterranean with our three young children, winter somewhere cheap in the south of Spain, then tour from campground to campground through Western Europe in the spring. We arranged to take the kids out of fifth, fourth, and second grades for a semester, rent out our little house in the countryside near the university, and sell our aging car. One problem remained: the family pets. The fish in the tropical fish tank, we explained to the children, would be "returned to the store"—and perhaps some were, although a memory haunts me of being discovered by my ten-year-old daughter in the act of flushing several down the toilet (*"Da-a-d!"*).

The cat was another matter. Survivor of a frisky pair of littermates named Nip and Tuck, the latter was a handsome three- or

four-year-old dear to all of us since his kittenhood. Except that his
coat was smoky gray instead of black, his markings resembled those
of that Baltimore casualty: tidy white bib, nose-blaze, and forepaw-
tops. Taking him with us by crowded camperbus through a dozen
foreign countries was out of the question, likewise imposing him on
friend or neighbor for half a year; and boarding him with a vet for
so long a period was beyond our straitened means. Anyhow, "Tucker
Jim," as the children called him, was used to roaming freely the rural
neighborhood and nearby woods; we couldn't imagine kenneling
him for months on end even if we could have afforded to. His similarly free-ranging sister had one day simply disappeared, perhaps
struck by a car on her country rambles, perhaps shot for sport by a
farm kid or a bored deer hunter (the venue here is the Alleghenies of
central Pennsylvania, where schools are closed for the opening day of
deer season and prudent parents keep children and pets grounded
till the fever abates). My then partner and I concurred that sometime
in this predeparture season dear Tuck must likewise officially disappear; as to the covert means, however, we disagreed, as alas we had
found ourselves lately doing on more and more matters of importance. She was all for having him "put to sleep"; I held out for turning
him loose a sufficient distance from home in the farm and forest
lands round about the state university where I then taught. That
would only condemn him to a slow and painful death instead of a
quick and painless one, she argued, and cited the SPCA's support of
her position. I didn't deny that possibility—although wily Tuck had
demonstrated his hunting skills on enough field mice and songbirds,
even while well fed at home, for me to doubt that starvation was a
likelihood in his case. My position was simply that in *his* position, if
offered those unpleasant alternatives, I would unhesitatingly opt to
take my chances in the wild.

What if you disappear him and we lie to the children and then he
finds his way back and we have to disappear him again?

Second time we'll tell them the truth. But I'll disappear him
good.

Do as you please. But you know what they say about cats.

I did, but, in this instance anyhow, did—not as I pleased, for it was no pleasure, but as I truly thought best: packed the chap into our up-for-sale station wagon one late October afternoon while the kids were in school; drove him a dozen miles over the Allegheny ridges, through forests of oak and hemlock, mountain laurel and rhododendron; chose a roadside spot where woods bordered corn and alfalfa fields, to give the guy some options (farmhouse and outbuildings just up the lane); grubstaked him with a paper bowl of 9 Lives cat food and another of milk in the dry ditch just off that lightly traveled road; sincerely wished him the best of luck . . . and drove away, returning home by a fairly extensive loop rather than directly. I wince at the memory of that evening's charade of gradually mounting concern, and the next day's and the next (*Where's old Tuck? Still hasn't come home?*); of the children's calling and combing the neighborhood, and my mate's low-volume after-their-bedtime reproaches (*I keep seeing him* out there *somewhere, meowing for us.*) (*You'd rather see him chloroformed and tossed into the vet's incinerator?*) (*Yes! Yes.*); and of my multiple burden of guilt, shared concern for the animal's welfare and the children's sorrow, and complex apprehension that Tuck might find his way home after all.

He didn't. The family's half-year European sojourn was of a value surely worth the sacrifice. Three dozen autumns later, I still stand by my course of action in l'affaire Tuck and, less firmly, the parental cover-up as well (Would it have been better overall to tell children aged ten, nine, and seven that we were in effect dumping a virtual family member in order to make the trip? They would have pleaded with us to spare him and stay home; we would have been obliged either to override their tearful protests or to present them with a fairly brutal fait accompli . . .). Other much-loved cats and dogs and tropical fish followed our return; other cars, houses, and universities in other states as those children floated, sometimes bumpily, into and through their adolescence, and their parents ever more rockily through the terminal stages of their once-happy union—which ended as the offspring one by one sprang off to college.

Such things happen.

Did I ever tell them, it occurred to me to wonder now in these dead-cat notes, what really happened to Tucker Jim? They're older these days than their father was in those, and presumably could handle the Truth. Am I, perhaps, telling them for the first time here? (How would *you* have handled it, mes enfants? Those of you especially who've had pets and children and marital vicissitudes of your own?) I wonder, for that matter, what really *did* happen to the good gray puss: that prolonged and wretched death foretold by my ex, the abundantly blessed next life-chapter enjoyed by *her* ex, or something between? Look here, Tuck boy, you still float through my memory thirty-six years later, now and then: Of how many cats can that be said?

(*Big deal,* I imagine him meowing: *You* ditched *me, man. Literally.*) (*But hey, it was either that or . . .*) (*Yeah, right: Lucky Tuck.*)

Where are you now, fellow? Where are those freshfaced children smiling gamely from my photos of *Europe 1962/63?* The snows and roses of yesteryear, *ubi sunt?* Where, for that matter, this shorter while later, is that leotarded lass en route to yogaland, who in a different story might have been a Cute Meet indeed? Where now is the cat corpse I bagged and dumped on her lissome behalf, where the briefly stymied talester who dumped it, that house in that city, and the life itwith involved? One *knows* where, to be sure, in a general way (*See So-and-So's 101 Uses for a Dead Cat,* recommends the still-prowling sardonic ghost of Tucker Jim)—but where are they all *exactly,* as I put this question?

That, too, in some instances at least, deponent can report, and in one case will: We being both of us newly retired from teaching and its attendant life-rhythms—which in our case had for many years involved busily straddling the Chesapeake between our "teaching house" in town and our weekend/summer retreat on Maryland's Eastern Shore—during a second trial Floridian winter Down There with the other Snowbird pensioners, my wife and I judged our urban base to be no longer earning its keep and arranged its sale to another, younger schoolteaching couple. During that same winter, as it happened, we were recalled north from sunny Geezerville on the unhappy errand of assisting the transfer of an aged parent, Alzheimer's-cursed, into a New Jersey nursing home for the closing chapter of her life-story. We stopped over in Baltimore, to begin preparing the

Teaching House for springtime occupancy by its new owners. The two businesses each melancholied the other, sharply reminding us of our own new life-stage and ongoing drift down Time's nontidal river. And in course of inspecting the house's exterior and grounds— refastening a storm-loosened shutter, picking car-tossed litter from the streetside shrubs—I came upon the second sequel to that dead cat nonadventure: on our front lawn, down near the seldom-used sidewalk of that traffic arterial, just a few dozen car-lengths from its predecessor . . . *another dead cat,* this one so flattened by traffic before being somehow shifted from street to lawn (perhaps by snow-plows), and so weathered and decomposed in our absence, that without examining the corpse more closely than I cared to I couldn't judge its sex or even quite its fur-color. Indeed, so virtually merged was it with the winter lawn, it seemed more the imprint or basso-relievo of a cat than the former animal itself.

A calling card, it amused me to imagine, from Ms. Lotus Position, as—who knows?—perhaps the first had been: the 102nd Use, her kinky way of striking up a potential new relationship, starting a new story. *Still there, Mr. Good Samaritan? Still interested?*

No and yes, Ma'am'selle: Your GS doesn't live here any more, practically speaking, but (disinterestedly) interested he remains— not in your shapely self, thanks, but in this all-but-shapeless souvenir, so desiccated past disgust that I let it rest in peace where it lay, reasonably confident that by spring lawn-mowing time it would be recycled altogether.

As in fact it proved to be except in the recirculating tide of my imagination, where it remained a floating touchstone. Two months later, over late-March wine and cheese at our last cocktail-time in the Teaching House before the movers came to shift us from the city for keeps, Maybe it was old Tuck, I proposed to my wife: It took him thirty-six years, but the cat came back. Tracked me all the way from that life to this one, he did, from Pennsylvania to upstate New York and Massachusetts and then back here to Maryland, and just as he was dragging his weary old bones down the last city block to this house, the Cat Lady nailed him with her cat-gray Honda.

Cute em-ee-*ay*-tee, replied my patient partner, and we touched

wineglasses in a sober toast to Time: It spared him the disappointment of finding you not home.

Tuck would've waited me out, I declared, or tracked me to Florida
or the Eastern Shore. What's thirty-six years, after all? It took *me* that
long to get from where I was then to where I am now.

Mm hm. And where is that, exactly?

Good question, beloved sharer of my life-story and reader of these
lines, to whom I respond as to myself: Why, where that is exactly is
at the floating point of this pen as it writes *at the floating point of this
pen;* it's at the track of your eye as your eye tracks the words *the words*
in this final sequel to or reprise of that now-disincarnate cat, in its
decomposition composed at last.

(*Sez you,* comes back the ghost of Tucker Jim. For even as there
are touchstone images that the narrative use of far from exhausts;
that when we believed we had done them with not only continue to
float or prowl upon their uncomprehended way but return, return to
tease or spook us, so there are stories, Reader, this theme among, that
hopefully substitute the sonority of closure for the thing itself; that
may *sound* done but are not; that, like an open parenthesis, without
properly ending at least for the cross-fingered present stop.

ALAN CHEUSE

Counting Forward, Counting Back

Ten—
Nine—
Eight—
Seven—
Six—
Five—
Four—
Three—
Two—
One—
Ignition!

The blast, the fiery light, the cloud arises, unfolds, that huge white-and-grey mushroom on a stalk of flame. . . .

Dr. J. Robert Oppenheimer, one of the creators of this new and deadly fire, watched from the observation bunker as the first atomic cloud spilled upwards into the heavens and quoted from the *Bhagavad Gita*— "I am Death, Destroyer of Worlds. . . ."

And that was that, some people between the ages of twenty-five and forty were saying to me as we sat around a table and talked about the idea of progress one recent bright autumn day when the air was so warm and the sun so present that it seemed as though time and the season might be preserved forever in amber. Over the course of this conversation, most of them claimed that their notion of progress as a positive force in the world had disintegrated along with all of the New Mexico rocks and sand at Alamogordo, an event that most of them knew only from news reels and history books.

"Personal progress, that's all we have left," one of them said, a personable young woman in her late twenties with a bent for reading great literature and writing about it, a profession to which one can adhere, ironically enough, if one has only the greatest amount of optimism about the future of the job market.

"That's right," another student said, this fellow a family man, dark skinned, hard working, teaching public school by day and doing graduate work by night. "You can inch along, but you can't leap anymore. Those days are over."

They were convincing in that moment, so convincing that I sat there for a while at my end of the table wondering why my own sense of progress hadn't been destroyed in that blast. I had every reason to let it go. Wasn't I a first-generation child of the Atomic Age? My burgeoning sense of progress could easily have slipped away from me in the musty classrooms of School No. 7 in Perth Amboy, New Jersey, soon after that first poisonous mushroom cloud billowed up into the stratosphere. At the same time the teachers imbued me with my sense of American possibilities ("one nation, with liberty and justice for all"), they also taught us to duck beneath our desks at the sound of a siren or, if caught out in the dark hallways, to fold ourselves into fetal balls, one arm covering our faces, the other covering our heads. Death could descend on us in a pillar of fire at home while we ate or slept. But at school we were prepared.

Maybe this sense of false security helped me to fend off somehow that threat of instantaneous nuclear annihilation. Or maybe because of all of the propaganda and idealistic musings mixed with hype about the wonders of modern science, I never associated that explosion until much later with the dangers of science. Along with Stanley Kubrick's Dr. Strangelove we all, in some bizarre and disconcerting way, learned to love the Bomb.

It's easy to understand why that happened. The positive nature of progress was our creed as Americans ("one nation, indivisible . . .")

and had been since the inception of our country. And in history classes at the university I learned that the twentieth century was the American century and that the idea of progress had become our anthem. All my living and reading after that confirmed for me that we were living in the age of the new, a century of marvelous new inventions, new medicine, new technology, new modes of painting, of writing—from *Ulysses* and cubism to the fax machine (actually predicted by Jules Verne in his novel *Life in the Twentieth Century,* written in 1861 though unpublished until 1996) to the probes of the far rim of the solar system. If fear of the atomic bomb was great, most of the time we repressed it, preferring to crow to ourselves about the great forward leaps in modern life.

We've all seen those movies, the assured voice-over about the inventions that are going to change the way we live, from self-cleaning houses to automobiles powered by solar panels. The moon landings. The Mars landing. Surveyor. Our eye on the outer planets. This is our world, this will be our future. We kept those voice-overs in our heads. News about the great advances in medicine, about battery-powered automobiles, portable telephones, faxes, beepers, miniature television sets, car phones, the compact disc, the laser, the laser disc, the heart pump, the hydraulic penis, the heart valve, the CD-ROM, the Mars Rover, the Jupiter probe, e-mail, synthetic insulin and the birth control pill, color printers, the pacemaker, the Net. . . . I believed all that. I believed that we could make great progress in communicating with one another across great distances. We ended totalitarianism in our time. We brought down the wall. Science played a role in this. Why else would the Communists have kept all their xerox machines under lock and key? Science and freedom go hand in hand. Science frees the word. Science frees the mind.

I had personal, if minor, testimony to give on this score. Three years ago I worked on an electronic typewriter and had been doing so for nearly ten years after the demise of my electric typewriter, mother of five books of my own and three of my ex-wife's, who gave the machine to me when she bought a computer (causing me to give up my manual machine). Then I began using a computer, and I haven't looked back.

"It's like going from a bicycle to a Mercedes," I heard myself saying to friends, amazed at my decision, for the first year or so that I
was using it. How could I have ignored such a leap forward in useful
technology? The same epoch that brought us the A-bomb made it
easier for me to type and edit my work. This is technological progress
at its most beneficent. Do I duck under my desk and place one arm
across my face and the other over my neck before I begin to write each
day? No, no, the A-bomb and global warming and all of the other
horrors wrought by modern technological life seem too far away
from my daily round for me to care much about them.

But lately we have seen technology, particularly modern medicine, falter and even fail us in ways far too close to home for us to ignore, mainly in the wake of the worldwide AIDS epidemic and in
medicine's uphill battle against a plethora of mutated microbes—
mean, nasty, disease-creating bugs for whom *progress* means rapidly
making themselves immune to most of our so-called wonder drugs.
And the cause of this problem? Medicine itself—too many doctors
overprescribing or incorrectly prescribing the very antibiotics that
modern chemistry has made it possible for the drug companies to
produce.

The hitch in the stride of the great forward movement of conventional medicine reminded me that the idea of progress has not always
been with us. Nothing like it obtained in preclassical antiquity. The
Greeks knew cycles, not progressive incremental change. As the British philosopher-historian J. B. Bury pointed out in his 1932 book-
length essay *Idea of Progress,* it was the Hebraic vision of a tribe sin-
gled out by a judgmental God as His primary agent for change in
time that first introduced this paradigm into the world. With the
idea of change in history suddenly apparent, things were ripe for the
advent of Christianity, which put out the call that all people could
change their situations in time by accepting Christ as their personal
savior—do this and a better time, eternity as opposed to mere human time, looms in your future.

So the idea of an advance in time as an advance in quality comes
to us from theology, from the quest to find a better world than this.
The actual use of the verb *to progress* in association with this idea,

however, is a rather late development. For many hundreds of years *to progress* meant only to move forward or advance in a physical fashion. From the Renaissance to the eighteenth century people used the word as a synonym for *parade*. I like that usage a lot. Worms make a progress through Polonius's guts, Hamlet tells us. Human progress made the picture in mind of row upon row of marchers, in the front ranks the latest human beings on earth; bringing up the rear, all of those who have come before.

The figurative use of the word as a way of describing an advance to a higher stage or better condition enters the language only in the seventeenth century. Look, for example, at the title of John Bunyan's famous allegory, published in 1678, about a Christian traveler in a world of despair: *The Pilgrim's Progress, from this world, to that which is to come.* Two hundred years pass and we find that science has appropriated the word in order to describe the betterment of the human condition. In the twentieth century left-wing politicians took up the word as well. What am I? I am a *progressive.* I believe in a political system that can make a better world.

I believed it. Almost all of it. A-bomb or no A-bomb, science could improve our lives beyond measure. I knew that. I celebrated it. In my house I have gadgets and services that make me in many ways richer than kings of old. And it's not just in the physical world of science that I can improve. I can undergo spiritual and psychological change. As the wonderfully naïve and optimistic Dale Carnegie system for self-betterment used to have its practitioners chant, "Every day, in every way, I am getting better and better."

Sort of.

My efforts as a writer, teacher, father, and husband have all, I think, improved over the days and years. (My work at being a friend, citizen, and enemy has probably deteriorated somewhat.) Overall, I may have made some progress as a human being. And as an artist.

And yet, as I've always been, I'm still parading toward the grave.

That's the tragic paradox lurking in the seemingly solid and attractive secular idea of progress. Having found its origins in the Christian conception of a place better than this, an afterworld toward which one can strive and hope some day to achieve, the notion of worldly progress presumes that we can all make this earth of ours better within the scope of human time—a paradise erenow. With one fatal catch. Anyone who works for it will only stick around for less than a hundred years, some considerably less.

So maybe what those folks were expressing in that autumnal conversation illuminated by that brilliant light was their disappointment that progress could not make them immortal. I'm quite disappointed in that, too, I have to admit.

But still I remain a firm believer in the idea of progress, for all its complexity. What else can you believe if you try to write novels? The second draft must be better than the first draft, the third must improve upon the second, the fourth prove better than the third. The process reminds me of the labor of the gods in the creation myth at the beginning of the Quiche Maya creation story, the *Popul-Vuh.* The gods first make the world and populate it with creatures made of paper. Fire burns them up. Next they make people out of clay. But rain washes them away. After a while the gods get the hang of it and create human beings, fragile, yes, but not as fragile as paper or clay.

If it took the gods of Middle America four cycles of creation to get it right, why should a novelist believe that he can work any faster?

We find one, two, three, four, five, perhaps sometimes even ten drafts, in the writer's struggle to reach that moment of ignition in which the illusory world on the page sparks to life. This count forward seems to me to stand as a wonderful counterpoint to the numerical descent from ten to zero toward a world in which science and destruction go hand in hand.

So there are a number of different ways to understand the meaning of progress in a world in which a count forward also leads toward the end and euphemisms such as "senior citizen" (jargon from the realm of the "social services," that legacy of the progressive politics of our century) mask the deterioration and winnowing away of spirit, muscle, and bone. But metaphor sometimes can act as a valuable shield against the ironic forward tending of progress toward the grave. Flimsy poetry, mortal fiction, evanescent dance, delicate paintings—these are some of the only answers we have in the face of relentless forward motion in a world without a belief in immortality.

Poetry, as Frost once wrote, is a momentary stay against confusion. I think he used that word *confusion* in a deep, deep way, meaning chaos and whorl. Under the sway of impersonal technological progress, and moving toward a millennium in which we can only see more of the same, our feeble gestures at making art appear, in their very fragility, an immense and daring act. These flowers, these songs, we offer up amidst the countdown toward oblivion, and the best of them reveal themselves to be, in their own way, brighter than a thousand suns.

NICHOLAS DELBANCO

Less and More

As my title suggests, this essay deals with linkage and could well have been called "More and Less." Or "Less or More" or "More is Less"; it's the conjunction of the words I wish to focus on, not the disjunction between them: two comparative terms in one breath. "More or less" is the common expression, of course—a way of indicating approximate accuracy—and it approximates my meaning, as does the aesthetic pronouncement, so famous in our modern age, that "less is more." The point, at least provisionally and at least for openers, is that "less and more" belong together; they've been joined at the titular hip.

And the burden of these pages will be to reverse expectation—so that "more" need not loom larger in its hierarchical connotation than "less." We build our structures from the bottom up; the narrow apex of a triangle requires the broad base. The crowning glory of a cupola or spire would have little value or importance at ground level, and managerial techniques now emphasize the lateral not vertical arrangement; the superannuated executive will likely get "kicked upstairs." Yet we "strip for action" and "get down to brass tacks"; parable and fable both insist that the higher we tower the harder we fall. According to the story, a bending reed outlasts the storm that killed a mighty oak. Time and again in the natural world the diminutive creature surpasses the large; the dinosaur is but a memory where cockroaches endure.

Sideways motion equally may represent advance. Not all progress is predictable or regular; change comes in fits and starts. Nor is the ranking absolute; the terms aren't "most and least." So perhaps our proper figure is not a triangle or pyramid but the circle and the sphere. The mighty rolling wheel of industry and the engines of advancement could be drawn instead as Fortune's Wheel, with a cautionary warning that the prosperous will come undone and the proud man topple. If it's true that what goes up comes down and that every action engenders a reaction, then the dialectic offers us our dance step: *one forward, one back, sideways slide.* We start dying with each newborn breath, and Shakespeare's "second childhood"—the last stage of the pilgrimage described in *As You Like It*—replicates the first. Perhaps the wheel's hub, spoke, and rim are one within this turning world: both less and more amounting not so much to progress as the zero sum.

Last winter I made a quick trip to Vermont and that southwest portion of the state I called, for decades, home. It was ice raddled, bone-chillingly cold, and not easy to negotiate the hills. But one of the things that I did on the trip was pay a visit to a friend, a woman now nearly one hundred years old who's been immobilized by snow; she told me that for six weeks running she's left the house only to go the doctor or when someone offers to drive.

Those offers come infrequently; she's in an old people's home. It's a common story: widowhood, infirmity, then the doctor's strong suggestion that she shouldn't live alone. Next a couple of falls in a bathtub and the collective decision that supervised living is best. Her large family has long ago moved elsewhere; her children themselves are too old to care for her properly, her grandchildren otherwise engaged, her great grandchildren too young. There are seventeen of them, by recent count, and the inexorable arithmetic of population—a kind of exponential increase derived from that aged single stem. There's a family photograph propped by her bed in which she

sits surrounded by some thirty-odd descendants: all smiling, all saying "Cheese."

I'm not one of them, not a relative. But in absolute terms she
matters to me and my wife; she took care of our two daughters way
back when. We've been close for twenty years. So I try not to go to
that part of the world without stopping by to visit, to bring her news
and flowers and wave the gossip flag. For though her physical agility
has lessened, though she walks with a cane and uses a hearing aid,
there's no real diminution of her mental faculties: this woman—
let's call her Harriet—is tack-sharp still. She wants to be out in the
world.

And after mud season it's possible; from late spring through autumn it's fine. She can visit her hairdresser, maybe, or meet a friend
in restaurants, or have a grandchild take her touring just to see the
sights. But mobility's an issue in winter; the white house where
they've put her sits at the top of a high hill, then down a long un-
plowed drive. And there's no money for road maintenance; the care-
taker is careful with both salt and sand. He plows the place from time
to time—enough to make certain that he can get through. But that's
about the size of it, and few others manage: the five old people interred in the house drink soup and masticate sandwiches and sit and
sleep and watch television and, outside, the snow.

So I take my rented car and barrel through. The doorbell is broken, the front door unlocked. I've called ahead; she's waiting, and
we settle in. "My, my," she says, "you're a sight for sore eyes," but
what she wants to talk about is trouble, not good news. Harriet
complains about the staff, the owners, the company, the food. When
she lived down in the village her house was full of visitors, and she
produced the best sticky buns and oyster stew from Brattleboro to
Rutland. She was famous for her popovers and jam. These days she's
losing weight; each night she looks down at her plate and says, "Oh
no, oh not again." Though she's precisely as old as the century, she
feels like a hundred and five. She can't even go to church. She was late
for her doctor's appointment last week, and when the nurse said,
"Better late than never," Harriet had disagreed. "Don't blame me,"

she said. "When I was on my own two feet I never was a single minute late."

So I say how things are hard, how the world feels like the weather and things keep on slipping downhill. Harriet looks up at me. She shakes her white head; she adjusts her teeth. "There's more truth than poetry in that," she says. I ask her to repeat the phrase; she does. "There's more truth than poetry in that."

Yet the currency great poets coin is truth. "Time's thievish progress to eternity," as Shakespeare wrote, looms inescapable. And most of us grow used, in one way or another, to those transactions that pass the time—that mark the "thievish progress" from youth to middle age. Gain and loss are kissing cousins; it's hard to grow up without growing old, or move to a new place without leaving something behind. There are often compensations in such changes—of towns, say, or countries or consorts. You lose a child and get grandchildren, you gain in gravity while gaining weight; you shift politics or clothing styles or jobs.

These are year-end reflections, likely as not—attached to that grim reaper we now call Father Time. According to the Orphics, our Hallmark note card image of a graybeard with a blade has a more edgy origin—having to do with an oracle that warned the great God Ouranos he would be supplanted by his son. So the fierce creature ate his progeny in order to protect himself, as in Francisco Goya's nightmarish image of that bearded Titan swallowing his seed. But Mother Gaea hid and saved her best-beloved Kronos, serving up a rock for supper and keeping her favorite child. When Kronos grew up, and up to the task, he took a scythe and cut off his father's genitals, thereby assuming dominion—at least until his own boy Zeus did much the same. This Greek parable was adopted by the Romans with an adaptive spelling change; Kronos is spelled with a *K,* but they recorded it as Chronos instead. This latter spelling has to do with the Greek root for time, as in *chronology* and *chronometry,* and the ambitious boy got transmuted in the telling to graybeard Father Time. So that's what the Grim Reaper really means and why he wields a sickle and what he slices off—not the green stalk of the old year, since in our northern latitudes not much grows in December.

When a doctor says, "You must take these pills; you must stop smoking or drinking or wear a pacemaker," we tend to take such injunctions seriously indeed. When an employer says "You're fired" or the voting public votes you out of office or a manager tells you you won't make the team, it's food for remedial thought. There are happy occasions for change also, of course, and these are the ones that we tend to call progress: we win the lottery or pennant, we get selected by Publisher's Clearinghouse to take a vacation in Tahiti, we discover that an ice-cream flavor we patented ten years ago is now the nation's rage. . . .

Most of the time, however, our life shifts are less seismic—a little sideways motion, a small alteration of emphasis, a line crossed that we fail to notice till we're on the other side. We formalize the solstice, but winter blends to spring. Or take the annual party we so avidly look forward to, then one year come to think of as an annual bore. A new job, a new coat grows old. The child who scrutinizes his or her reflection in the mirror daily cannot see how large a change the year-end visitor perceives: "How much we've grown," shrieks Aunt Elsie or Uncle Bert, while inwardly we shrink. Time-lapse photography has made of mutation an art form: plants thrust up from the frozen earth, unfold, flower and fade and disappear in the act of compressed extended witness; so too with our faces and shapes. Consider the family album: a child in nursery school, then summer camp, then at college commencement, then the twenty-fifth reunion photograph and eightieth birthday celebration, and the passage of time is made plain.

The elders of far northern tribes go out onto the ice, I'm told, when there's insufficient food remaining for those who still might live. Between the example of peremptory dismissal provided by young Kronos and the example of such sacrifice there must be some room to maneuver, and here's where the time-lapse pertains. As though entropy and dis*solution* were a negative solution only, a forced occasion for change. Little by little, inch by inch and day by

year things alter—and that's what occasions acknowledge: a thir-
teenth birthday, a twenty-first, a wedding anniversary, a golden ju-
bilee. . . .

Long ago I bought and lived in and slowly remodeled a brick farmhouse not far distant from the place where Harriet still sits. Rock
Hill—as it was called on old surveyors' maps—dated from 1820 or
so, and it had been imposing once: Georgian, four chimneys, large
windowed, with a marble entry stoop worn concave from hard use.
The years had preserved but not treated it kindly; the house had the
usual assortment of "improvements"—which is to say six or seven
layers of wallpaper on the crumbled plaster, linoleum on the wide-
planked floor, bricked-up fireplaces and fake entries and stairwells
and secondary ceilings: the detritus of previous owners whose taste
mirrored previous styles. Then, at the stroke of a purchaser's pen, the
house became mine to renew.

Those were the days when restoration seemed less attractive than
renovation; there was little in the place we wanted to preserve. My
wife and I were young and ambitious, and together we gutted the
house. I laid about with a sledgehammer and wrecking bar and a
good deal of enthusiasm, and soon we had what felt like the only loft
within two hundred miles of Houston Street: open beams and exposed brick walls, unimpeded prospects of the stock pond and the
barn, a city dweller's dream of country life. But though we could as-
sist with what is now called "deconstruction," the reverse required
skill. "Construction" was beyond our competence, so we hired carpenters to put in plate glass windows and triple the size of the kitchen
and recess the lights. The center hall, for example, acquired an iron
spiral staircase; the four cramped downstairs rooms became one. It's
a familiar story: by the time the place had been transformed to our
entire liking we were ready to move on. Another family produced another checkbook; we shook hands and signed papers and left
town. . . .

So after I left the old people's home, and because I was back in the
neighborhood, I dropped by Rock Hill to say hello. "We're making

progress with the place," the owners told me happily; "we're gaining on it. Come and see." I went inside and had a cup of coffee and admired what they called their "progress" on the house. At some point in their tenancy the new owners have grown obsessed with authenticity—and now they are bound and determined to restore the building to its original state. Gone our beloved spiral stairwell; returned the entrance hall. Gone our recessed floodlights; returned the candleholder and the argand lamp. Gone the open fireplace; returned the period mantle. They've had a harpsichord maker carve the portico; the daguerreotypes upon the walls look like last season's family portraits. Even the books on the shelves were printed in the 1820s, or before; the flower beds display only flowers from the first part of last century, and when they get around to it they'll tear away the plumbing and restore the outhouse, too.

Their sense of tradition is as firmly fixed, in short, as was ours of innovation, and soon there'll be no more light switches or electric outlets or the zoned oil-fired furnace we took such pride in installing. And I felt as if I had witnessed a reel of film reversing, in which all things wound backwards to the opening credits and frame. They stop short of wearing costumes, but the wheel has entirely turned.

The house endures us all.

A recent study has informed us that Americans live longer yet again; our average life expectancy is now 76 years of age. Not long ago those digits were reversed; 67 years was what an American male could expect, and those whose memories are longer no doubt remember the number when less. It's a mixed blessing, as many of us have come to suspect; there's real irony in the tale of the Cumaean Sibyl, who asked for and received eternal life. But who forgot to ask, into the bargain, for eternal youth. And who withered and shriveled away, growing older and older, and whose only utterance was the repeated despairing cry: "I want to die."

Or think of Xeno's paradox—that if we continually halve the distance towards an anticipated goal we never will attain it. There's a half left to begin with, then a quarter, then an eighth, a sixteenth, a thirty-second, and so on—but the end remains, if only infinitesimally, some distance and space still ahead. In this way we approach the Sibyl's problematic immortality: if for every year of life we gain another year of life expectancy, the population changes and the terms of the problem, too, change.

I don't mean to engage the present debate as to assisted suicide, or entitlement programs or health care delivery, but rather to point out the obvious: our youthful solutions grow old. In important ways, I think, we need to consider what all this entails in terms of the transfer of power—how one generation prepares to make way and give over to the next. The very word *generation* entails its own reversal; we generate and bring forth our biological replacement and get displaced and degenerate and move on. But there's a difference between doing so at age thirty or age eighty, and most of our models are closer to the former than the latter. It's the young artist we celebrate, the young athlete and entrepreneur and politician, not to mention "model"—and as long as the natural course of things kept Keats or Mozart or Alexander the Great from growing old the question of what to do with old age simply wasn't as pressing to ask. "Bodily decrepitude is wisdom," writes Yeats, but our collective wisdom on the subject seems at present scant.

We have, in America, a great many books and a good deal of advice on how to succeed, how to acquire prominence, and then to maintain and increase it—instructions of all sorts on self-improvement. It's a national obsession, nearly, whether we're talking about bankbooks or golf games or biceps, whether the subject is big business or politics or entertainment or health. And such instruction manuals almost always take for granted the notion of increase and plenty, that power is ours for the taking or making, and that more will be more. The reverse is a proposition too few of us focus on and that all of us—consciously or no—must wrestle with, if only in terms of how to deal with what is certain: taxes, death. Just think how much more frequent is the usage of the meliorist word *progress* than that of its opposite, *regress;* the latter term sounds foreign and even a degree unnatural to the American ear.

For it sometimes seems harder to give up an office than gain it, to dispense a fortune than acquire it, to retire than continue to entertain or play. Often a person is voted out of office, of course, or gets fired or goes broke or fails to attract an audience—but these are examples of *involuntary* retirement. In Western civilization the idea of *voluntary* retirement has been almost exclusively attached to the religious life; we go behind the convent wall or kneel on the monk's floor to pray. The prince who chooses to be pauper does so for spiritual gain. And the answers so much a part of other cultures (the Buddhist model of renunciation, the Hindu of withdrawal) are at best an uneasy fit with present Western ways.

Imagine if the pope chose to retire, or Queen Elizabeth passed on the crown to her heir apparent, or the founder of a business empire arranged an orderly transition—and the point may come more clear. Whether our national dream be that of the gold rush and streets paved with gold or, more modestly, a car in each garage and a chicken in every pot, the notion of America is ineluctably linked to the idea of forward motion, the ideals of self-help, self-improvement, self-reliance, and the rest. And much of our current malaise, perhaps, can be attributed to the recognition that not all problems can be solved, not all resources prove inexhaustible, and not all frontiers can be pushed back without damage. "Manifest destiny," in this reading, means to keep on keeping on.

Yet Janus is a two-faced god, with eyes in front and eyes behind: the one who gives his name to January and looks both forward and back. What we require, both individually and collectively, are models for that backward face: the willing withdrawal from power, for when to say "enough's enough," and how to live with less.

A good number of characters in early novels—by which I mean those of the eighteenth and nineteenth centuries—have, as it were, "great expectations," or are "living on a competence" or have been left substantial or small legacies by a distant uncle or a maiden aunt. They don't seem to work for a living; they are eligible or marriageable in more or less direct proportion to the size of their estate. In part, perhaps, this comes about because the authors of those novels would therefore need to focus less on the workaday world and could concern themselves exclusively with the inner emotional life of their characters; if you don't spend time on the nine to five, there's more space for heart and mind. But one cannot escape the suspicion that—at least in terms of fiction—more people used to inherit more than is the case today. Or at least they did so *earlier;* there are all those fortunate gentlemen or fortune hunters and ladies with cocked hats or dowries festooning all those pages in Austen, Balzac, and the rest.

Lately I've come to understand that this has something to do with actuarial tables; if you come into your inheritance at sixty because the maiden aunt or foreign uncle dies in their eighties or nineties it's less romantic by far. Tax laws too have altered; you can't give a kingdom away or simply designate an heir apparent and offer up the throne. Prince Charming gets long in the tooth and Cinderella gets dishpan hands if you make them wait too many years before they acquire bequests; Rumpelstiltskin could turn straw to gold but one point of his story is that he was a bitter old man. It is, of course, the case that most of us have no inheritance or expectation of a life-altering legacy; the vast majority of people don't rely for their own living on what someone leaves. But the novel is a middle-class art form, a description of society organized by commerce, and it's not, I think, an accident that characters with trust funds are less populous in today's pages than were their equivalents two centuries ago.

Shakespeare's tragedy *King Lear* takes as its occasion the old man's decision, at play's start, to give up his absolute power and give everything away. He wants his children to praise and then take care of him, and according to how loudly they sing his praises he will divide his estate. Two of his daughters are hypocrites and flatter the choleric king; the youngest, who truly loves him, has nothing public to say. "Nothing will come of nothing," rages the old man famously, and what in fact comes of his decision to disinherit his darling Cordelia is general catastrophe—the madness on the heath, the kingdom in collapse. But the reading I'd propose is not that Lear stay on his throne but that he offer it up to the *correct* daughter: in which case there'd have been no trouble or, of course, the tragedy itself. It's a kind of estate planner's guide, a warning about poor investments and insufficient scrutiny of the company you choose; make certain that you mean it when you allocate bequests.

What I'm trying to describe is the widespread fear—and it would seem to be the first time we've felt this way—that prosperity is on the wane and not around the corner, that we'll be lucky as a general rule to do as well in America as did our parents, and that our children face a future less lavish than the present. In our image of the self or family or nation, the prospect of increase and plenty no longer seems to prevail. Whether the yardstick be economic or ecological, whether the enemy stands without or within, there's a sense that progress best describes the storied past and that the epoch to come will not belong to our nation as much as the one nearly done.

Such pervasive unease may be a necessary corrective, in fact, since not all streets are paved with gold and the pot of it at rainbow's end isn't that easy to find. But think of all those heroines and heroes whose history was organized by "great expectations" and you'll see how the rising dawn of this country's great day was mirrored in, reflected by our literature. The happy ending was the rule; by now it's the exception. The girl in Rumpelstiltskin's tower too grows old with spinning, and the princess kisses an imprisoned creature who remains a frog. That "nothing will come of nothing" turns out to be, alas, the dark commercial truth.

On the French slope of the Pyrenees, beneath the high, snow-crested triangular peak of Mount Canigou, stands an abbey constituted more than a thousand years ago: San Miguel de Cuxa. The names are Catalan, the monks are Benedictine, and there are very few of them remaining: five or six. They tend sheep and sell wine and cheese and peach preserves and flowers; from time to time they make visitors welcome, and last month my wife and I—along with an international contingent of cellists—called the monastery home.

Cuxa has a famed history; it was founded near the village of Codalet on the nineteenth of June, 879. It rapidly became a place of learning, consequential disputation, and power in retreat. At the urging of Abbot Garin, the Venetian Doge Pietro Orseola journeyed west in 978 and remained in Cuxa till his death. In the eleventh century Orseola was canonized and his skull interred beneath the altar, but during his lifetime—since he had not taken orders and could not sleep within the walls—the saint slept outside, on rock. The shape of his body, or so the locals like to say, is imprinted on the soft stone paving where the vineyard starts. Our own accommodations proved rather better: a pallet on wood planking, a cross and no mirrors on the wall, a communal bathroom three corridors away, with the only sound the monks at matins or the cellists in their practice rooms behind the low refectory where, three times a day, we ate.

There's a beautiful Lombard steeple, an eleventh-century crypt, and the remains of a grandiose cloister built in the twelfth century. That structure itself did not survive the French Revolution or its leveling zeal in the name of equality; more than a hundred years thereafter, John Rockefeller gathered stored rocks from a warehouse in the region and constructed his medieval "Cloisters"—with capitals from Cuxa—on New York's Washington Heights.

In America the reach of history is short and, by and large, within our grasp. There are ancient buildings and burial sites on this continent also, of course, but such a structure as the Abbey of San Miguel de Cuxa is unimaginable unless purchased by a millionaire a millennium after the fact. To watch the monks trim fruit trees or the farmer spread manure, to see how snowmelt off the mountains has been channeled to the vineyards and hear the bells of grazing sheep is to witness constancy in change. And in this time of accelerating change, of future-facing prophets and exponentially increased information, it's lovely beyond simple saying to withdraw to a place where the world is as it was. Nor did it feel so much like a retreat as an advance: the threat of invasion came only from a tourist bus, the wells had not been poisoned, and the single telephone rang in a booth in a field. . . .

The reader will have noticed that this essay has two modes. One set of entries is personal, one impersonal; the former consists of memory and the latter of speculation. Those three descriptive anecdotes (my old friend, my old house, the Benedictine abbey that became the Cloisters) bear only a tangential relation to the straight line of "progress"; they engage it indirectly if at all. To face a ruin such as Cuxa—and, more mysteriously even, Stonehenge or the pyramids, Uxmal or

Angkor Wat—is to question in what ways we have advanced. That we *have* advanced as species is self-evident, I think, and what I blithely called a zero sum at the end of the first entry is blithely dismissive of rockets, democracy, inoculation, and the rest; more people inhabit the planet with pleasure than has been the case before. The *weight* of progress overwhelms; the sheer density of population, traffic jams, and personal computers that herald the developed world may tempt us to turn Luddite. Yet it's a temptation we ought to resist, since only those who live in plenty yearn to live with less. . . .

Now let me use my text as test and admit that in these pages I've been more than usually allusive. Or, one might argue, elusive. I've cited Goya, Gaea, Kronos, Chronos, Father Time, the Orphics, Shakespeare, Yeats, the Luddites, and so on. And perhaps the point was made and perhaps it's memorable and perhaps there are some readers who won't think the same way again about our figurative Grim Reaper. But I'd hazard the opinion that far more will remember—or would if I wrote it well enough—that scene about my visit to the woman in the snow. There was narrative there, a situation and dramatic sequence and an exchange in dialogue. There was no single literary allusion, however, or quotation or citation, just a middle-aged man in a rented car who visits an old people's home. . . .

But in that passage possibly I clarified as not elsewhere the fact of long life and its insult to flesh, the way we are imprisoned soon or late by immobility. And this is what the novelist does, or tries to do when making scenes: create an image of the world in words that reflects and, when we close our eyes or close the book, refracts it. If the reader can remember the woman I've called Harriet, if I have conjured her successfully, then the question of whether or not she exists, whether or when I did take that trip, whether or not she said what I report her saying, "There's more truth than poetry in that," is, or should be, moot.

The root meaning of *progress,* according to *The Oxford English Dictionary,* has more to do with the physical action of movement than an abstract progressive ideal. It is, as suggested above, more literal than theoretical, more specific than abstract. The first meaning offered is "The action of stepping or marching forward or onward; onward march; journeying, travelling, travel; a journey, an expedition. (Now *rare*.)" The second definition has to do with nobility; kings and queens performed a "progress" while they made a visit of state. The third and fourth definitions have to do with "onward movement in space" and "forward movement in space" respectively, and it is only at the end of several columns of examples and several hundred years of usage that we approach the figurative definition: "To make progress; to proceed to a further or higher stage, or to further or higher stages continuously; to advance, get on; to develop; increase; usually to advance to better conditions, to go on or get on well, to improve continuously."

This shift from *progress* in the literal to *progress* in the figurative sense would seem to have occurred in that most hopeful of centuries, the eighteenth. Having won the Revolution and served his time as president, George Washington could write in 1796 that "Our country . . . is fast *progressing* in its political importance and social happiness" (italics mine). On the other side of the Atlantic, Mary Russell Mitford, the author of *Our Village,* would locate the term as not native: "In country towns . . . society has been progressing (if I may borrow that expressive Americanism) at a very rapid rate." By 1850 Herbert Spencer would insist that "Progress, therefore, is not an accident, but a necessity. . . . It is a part of nature."

And the great if misrepresented scientific basis for "progress" derives, of course, from Darwin. If you accept that apes breed men and that the species *Homo sapiens* is a higher form of nature, then the whole history of evolution has to do with forward motion; we come out of the Galapagos or the Great Barrier Reef and go, sooner or later, to school. Yet it does seem to be the case that the articulated ideal of "progress" is an "expressive Americanism"; although Lord Macaulay might announce in the 1830s that "The history of England is emphatically the history of progress," more often the term in its optimistic forward-facing aspect has been yoked to the New World.

But all such emphatic usage is, I think, besides the point. We should accept and celebrate the idea of diminution equally as progress, of withdrawal and recurrence so that less means, also, more. To know when to stop is as difficult—in love and business and life and warfare and environmental management and essays—as to know where to begin.

ANNIE DILLARD

The Wreck of Time

I

Ted Bundy, the serial killer, after his arrest, could not fathom the fuss. What was the big deal? David Von Drehle quotes an exasperated Bundy in *Among the Lowest of the Dead:* "I mean, there are *so* many people."

One R. Houwink, of Amsterdam, uncovered this unnerving fact: The human population of earth, arranged tidily, would just fit into Lake Windermere, in England's Lake District.

Recently in the Peruvian Amazon a man asked the writer Alex Shoumatoff, "Isn't it true that the whole population of the United States can be fitted into their cars?"

How are we doing in numbers, we who have been alive for this most recent installment of human life? How many people have lived and died?

"The dead outnumber the living, in a ratio that could be as high as 20 to 1," a demographer, Nathan Keyfitz, wrote in a 1991 letter to the historian Justin Kaplan. "Credible estimates of the number of people who have ever lived on the earth run from 70 billion to over

49

100 billion." Averaging those figures puts the total persons ever born at about 85 billion. We living people now number 5.8 billion. By these moderate figures, the dead outnumber us about fourteen to one. The dead will always outnumber the living.

Dead Americans, however, if all proceeds, will not outnumber living Americans until the year 2030, because the nation is young. Some of us will be among the dead then. Will we know or care, we who once owned the still bones under the quick ones, we who spin inside the planet with our heels in the air? The living might well seem foolishly self-important to us, and overexcited.

We who are here now make up about 6.8 percent of all people who have appeared to date. This is not a meaningful figure. These our times are, one might say, ordinary times, a slice of life like any other. Who can bear to hear this, or who will consider it? Are we not especially significant because our century is—our century and its nuclear bombs, its unique and unprecedented Holocaust, its serial exterminations and refugee populations, our century and its warming, its silicon chips, men on the moon, and spliced genes? No, we are not and it is not.

Since about half of all the dead are babies and children, we will be among the longest-boned dead and among the dead who grew the most teeth—for what those distinctions might be worth among beings notoriously indifferent to appearance and all else.

In Juan Rulfo's novel *Pedro Páramo,* a dead woman says to her dead son, "Just think about pleasant things, because we're going to be buried for a long time."

II

On April 30, 1991—on that one day—138,000 people drowned in Bangladesh. At dinner I mentioned to my daughter, who was then seven years old, that it was hard to imagine 138,000 people drowning.

"No, it's easy," she said. "Lots and lots of dots, in blue water."

* * *

The paleontologist Pierre Teilhard de Chardin, now dead, sent a dispatch from a dig. "In the middle of the tamarisk bush you find a red-brick town, partially exposed. . . . More than 3,000 years before our era, people were living there who played with dice like our own, fished with hooks like ours, and wrote in characters we can't yet read."

Who were these individuals who lived under the tamarisk bush? Who were the people Ted Bundy killed? Who was the statistician who reckoned that everybody would fit into Lake Windermere? The Trojans likely thought well of themselves, one by one; their last settlement died out by 1,100 B.C.E. Who were the people Stalin killed, or any of the 79.2 billion of us now dead, and who are the 5.8 billion of us now alive?

"God speaks succinctly," said the rabbis.

Is it important if you have yet died your death, or I? Your father? Your child? It is only a matter of time, after all. Why do we find it supremely pertinent, during any moment of any century on earth, which among us is topsides? Why do we concern ourselves over which side of the membrane of topsoil our feet poke?

"A single death is a tragedy, a million deaths is a statistic." Joseph Stalin, that connoisseur, gave words to this disquieting and possibly universal sentiment.

How can an individual count? Do we individuals count only to us other suckers, who love and grieve like elephants, bless their hearts? Of Allah, the Koran says, "Not so much as the weight of an ant in earth or heaven escapes from the Lord." That is touching, that Allah, God, and their ilk care when one ant dismembers another, or note when a sparrow falls, but I strain to see the use of it.

Ten years ago we thought there were two galaxies for each of us alive. Lately, since we loosed the Hubble Space Telescope, we have revised our figures. There are nine galaxies for each of us. Each galaxy harbors an average of 100 billion suns. In our galaxy, the Milky Way, there are sixty-nine suns for each person alive. The Hubble shows, says a report, that the universe "is at least 15 billion years old." Two galaxies, nine galaxies . . . sixty-nine suns, 100 billion suns—

These astronomers are nickel-and-diming us to death.

III

What were you doing on April 30, 1991, when a series of waves drowned 138,000 people? Where were you when you first heard the astounding, heartbreaking news? Who told you? What, seriatim, were your sensations? Whom did you tell? Did you weep? Did your anguish last days or weeks?

All my life I have loved this sight: a standing wave in a boat's wake, shaped like a thorn. I have seen it rise from many oceans, and I saw it rise from the Sea of Galilee. It was a peak about a foot high. The standing wave broke at its peak, and foam slid down its glossy hollow. I watched the foaming wave on the port side. At every instant we were bringing this boat's motor, this motion, into new water. The stir, as if of life, impelled each patch of water to pinch and inhabit this same crest. Each crest tumbled upon itself and released a slide of white foam. The foam's bubbles popped and dropped into the general sea while they were still sliding down the dark wave. They trailed away always, and always new waters peaked, broke, foamed, and replenished.

What I saw was the constant intersection of two wave systems. Lord Kelvin first described them. Transverse waves rise abaft the stern and stream away perpendicular to the boat's direction of travel. Diverging waves course out in a V shape behind the boat. Where the waves converge, two lines of standing crests persist at an unchanging angle to the direction of the boat's motion. We think of these as the boat's wake. I was studying the highest standing wave, the one nearest the boat. It rose from the trough behind the stern and spilled foam. The curled wave crested over clear water and tumbled down. All its bubbles broke, thousands a second, unendingly. I could watch the present; I could see time and how it works.

* * *

On a shore, 8,000 waves break a day. James Trefil, a professor of physics, provides these facts. At any one time, the foam from breaking waves covers between 3 and 4 percent of the earth's surface. This acreage of foam is equal to the entire continent of North America. By coincidence, the U.S. population bears nearly the same relation to the world population: 4.6 percent. The U.S. population, in other words, although it is the third largest population among nations, is as small a portion of the earth's people as breaking waves' white foam is of the sea.

"God rises up out of the sea like a treasure in the waves," wrote Thomas Merton.

We see generations of waves rise from the sea that made them, billions of individuals at a time; we see them dwindle and vanish. If this does not astound you, what will? Or what will move you to pity?

IV

One-tenth of the land on earth is tundra. At any time, it is raining on only 5 percent of the planet's surface. Lightning strikes the planet about a hundred times every second. The insects outweigh us. Our chickens outnumber us four to one.

One-fifth of us are Muslims. One-fifth of us live in China. And every seventh person is a Chinese peasant. Almost one-tenth of us live within range of an active volcano. More than 2 percent of us are mentally retarded. We humans drink tea—over a billion cups a day. Among us we speak 10,000 languages.

We are civilized generation number 500 or so, counting from 10,000 years ago, when we settled down. We are *Homo sapiens* generation number 7,500, counting from 150,000 years ago, when our species presumably arose; and we are human generation number 125,000, counting from the earliest forms of *Homo*.

Every 110 hours a million more humans arrive on the planet than die into the planet. A hundred million of us are children who live on the streets. Over a hundred million of us live in countries where we hold no citizenship. Twenty-three million of us are refugees. Sixteen million of us live in Cairo. Twelve million fish for a living from small boats. Seven and a half million of us are Uygurs. One million of us crew on freezer trawlers. Nearly a thousand of us a day commit suicide.

HEAD-SPINNING NUMBERS CAUSE MIND TO GO SLACK, the *Hartford Courant* says. But our minds must not go slack. How can we think straight if our minds go slack? We agree that we want to think straight.

Anyone's close world of family and friends composes a group smaller than almost all sampling errors, smaller than almost all rounding errors, a group invisible, at whose loss the world will not blink. Two million children die a year from diarrhea and 800,000 from measles. Do we blink? Stalin starved 7 million Ukrainians in one year, Pol Pot killed 1 million Cambodians, the flu epidemic of 1918 killed 21 or 22 million people . . . shall this go on? Or do you suffer, as Teilhard de Chardin did, the sense of being "an atom lost in the universe"? Or do you not suffer this sense? How about what journalists call "compassion fatigue"? Reality fatigue? At what limit for you do other individuals blur? Vanish? How old are you?

V

Los Angeles airport has 25,000 parking spaces. This is about one space for every person who died in 1985 in Colombia when a volcano erupted. This is one space for each of the corpses of more than two years' worth of accidental killings from leftover land mines of recent wars. At five to a car, almost all the Inuit in the world could park at LAX. Similarly, if you propped up or stacked four bodies to a car, you could fit into the airport parking lot all the corpses from the firestorm bombing of Tokyo in March 1945, or the corpses of Londoners who died in the plague, or the corpses of Burundians killed in civil war since 1993. But you could not fit America's homeless there, not even at twenty to a car.

Since sand and dirt pile up on everything, why does the world look fresh for each new crowd? As natural and human debris raises the continents, vegetation grows on the piles. It is all a stage—we know this—a temporary stage on top of many layers of stages, but every year a new crop of sand, grass, and tree leaves freshens the set and perfects the illusion that ours is the new and urgent world now. When Keats was in Rome, I read once, he saw pomegranate trees overhead; they bloomed in dirt blown onto the Colosseum's broken walls. How can we doubt our own time, in which each bright instant probes the future? In every arable soil in the world we grow grain over tombs—sure, we know this. But do not the dead generations seem to us dark and still as mummies, and their times always faded like scenes painted on walls at Pompeii?

How can we see ourselves as only a new, temporary cast for a long-running show when a new batch of birds flies around singing and new clouds move? Living things from hyenas to bacteria whisk the dead away like stagehands hustling between scenes. To help a living space last while we live on it, we brush or haul away the blowing sand and hack or burn the greenery. We are mowing the grass at the cutting edge.

VI

In northeast Japan, a seismic sea wave killed 27,000 people on June 15, 1896. Do not fail to distinguish this infamous wave from the April 30, 1991, waves that drowned 138,000 Bangladeshi. You were not tempted to confuse, conflate, forget, or ignore these deaths, were you?

On the dry Laetoli plain of northern Tanzania, Mary Leakey found a trail of hominid footprints. The three barefoot people—likely a short man and woman and child *Australopithecus afarensis*—walked closely together. They walked on moist volcanic tuff and ash. We have a record of those few seconds from a day about 3.6 million years ago—before hominids even chipped stone tools. More ash covered their footprints and hardened. Ash also preserved the pockmarks of the raindrops that fell beside the three who walked; it was a rainy day. We have almost ninety feet of the three's steady footprints intact. We do not know where they were going or why. We do not know why the woman paused and turned left, briefly, before continuing. "A remote ancestor," Leakey said, "experienced a moment of doubt." Possibly they watched the Sadiman volcano erupt, or they took a last look back before they left. We do know we cannot make anything so lasting as these three barefoot ones did.

After archeologists studied this long strip of record for several years, they buried it again to save it. Along one preserved portion, however, new tree roots are already cracking the footprints, and in another place winds threaten to sand them flat; the preservers did not cover them deeply enough. Now they are burying them again.

Jeremiah, walking toward Jerusalem, saw the smoke from the temple's blaze. He wept; he saw the blood of the slain. "He put his face close to the ground and saw the footprints of sucklings and infants who were walking into captivity" in Babylon. He kissed the footprints.

Who were these individuals? Who were the three who walked together and left footprints in the rain? Who was that eighteenth-century Ukrainian peasant the Baal Shem Tov, the founder of modern Hasidism, who taught, danced, and dug clay? He was among the generations of children of Babylonian exiles whose footprints on the bare earth Jeremiah kissed. Centuries later the Emperor Hadrian destroyed another such son of exile in Rome, Rabbi Akiba. Russian Christians and European Christians tried, and Hitler tried, to wipe all those survivors of children of exile from the ground of the earth as a man wipes a plate—survivors of exiles whose footprints on the ground I kiss, and whose feet.

Who and of what import were the men whose bones bulk the Great Wall, the 30 million Mao starved, or the 11 million children under five who die each year now? Why, they are the insignificant others, of course; living or dead, they are just some of the plentiful others. And you?

Is it not late? A late time to be living? Are not our current generations the important ones? We have changed the world. Are not our
heightened times the important ones, the ones since Hiroshima?
Perhaps we are the last generation—there is a comfort. Take the
bomb threat away and what are we? We are ordinary beads on a never
ending string. Our time is a routine twist of an improbable yarn.

We have no chance of being here when the sun burns out. There
must be something ultimately heroic about our time, something
that sets it above all those other times. Hitler, Stalin, Mao, and Pol
Pot made strides in obliterating whole peoples, but this has been the
human effort all along, and we have only enlarged the means, as have
people in every century in history. (That genocides recur does not
mean that they are similar. Each instance of human evil and each
victim's death possesses its unique history and form. To generalize,
as Cynthia Ozick points out, is to "befog" evil's specificity.)

Dire things are happening. Plague? Funny weather? Why are we
watching the news, reading the news, keeping up with the news?
Only to enforce our fancy—probably a necessary lie—that these are
crucial times, and we are in on them. Newly revealed, and I am in the
know: crazy people, bunches of them! New diseases, sways in power,
floods! Can the news from dynastic Egypt have been any different?

As I write this, I am still alive, but of course I might well have died
before you read it. Most of the archeologists who reburied hominid
footprints have likely not yet died their deaths; the paleontologist
Teilhard is pushing up daisies.

Chinese soldiers who breathed air posing for 7,000 individual
clay portraits—twenty-two centuries ago—must have thought it a
wonderful difference that workers buried only their simulacra then
so that their sons could bury their flesh a bit later. One wonders what
they did in the months or years they gained. One wonders what one
is, oneself, up to these days.

VII

Was it wisdom Mao Tse-tung attained when—like Ted Bundy—he
awakened to the long view?

"The atom bomb is nothing to be afraid of," Mao told Nehru. "China has many people. . . . The deaths of ten or twenty million people is nothing to be afraid of." A witness said Nehru showed shock. Later, speaking in Moscow, Mao displayed yet more generosity: he boasted that he was willing to lose 300 million people, half of China's population.

Does Mao's reckoning shock me really? If sanctioning the death of strangers could save my daughter's life, would I do it? Probably. How many others' lives would I be willing to sacrifice? Three? Three hundred million?

An English journalist, observing the Sisters of Charity in Calcutta, reasoned: "Either life is always and in all circumstances sacred, or intrinsically of no account; it is inconceivable that it should be in some cases the one, and in some the other."

One small town's soup kitchen, St. Mary's, serves 115 men a night. Why feed 115 individuals? Surely so few people elude most demographics and achieve statistical insignificance. After all, there are 265 million Americans, 15 million people who live in Mexico City, 16 million in greater New York, 26 million in greater Tokyo. Every day 1.5 million people walk through Times Square in New York; every day almost as many people—1.4 million—board a U.S. passenger plane. And so forth. We who breathe air now will join the already dead layers of us who breathed air once. We arise from dirt and dwindle to dirt, and the might of the universe is arrayed against us.

BRUCE DUFFY

The Rocket of Progress

I was the can-do child of a can-do time, a muscular, kiloton-wielding, unironic, rocket sled of a time. An Ask-Not time of Kennedy *viggar* when crew-cutted men in white drip-dry shirts with slide rules in their pockets—men like my own dad, I fancied—were sending fiery rockets into space, rockets with actual men in tinfoil suits and their own portable air conditioners.

Even if you weren't a kid then, it was a time of national genuflection before the altar of progress. Forget the fact that Sputnik and Yury Gagarin had beat us in these early laps, for we were going to assault it, space itself, then the moon and Mars, *because we were Americans and Americans always won.* I sure believed it. In fact, I was training to be a scientist, I thought—anyhow, a guy who, with slide-rule cool, could control things—control, of course, being the whole thing, like with Mission Control, radio control, or even the grinning, dynamic muscle control of Charles Atlas.

And who in those days wasn't in training for the great American blastoff? Looking like a small siege engine on its wooden tower, creaking and tottering as three husky AV boys wheeled it into the school auditorium, the TV was set up so five hundred kids could watch John Glenn in the first U.S. orbital mission, *T minus three minutes fifty-five seconds. . . .* And it was weird, if you thought about it, that we *counted backward so the future could go roaring forward.*

But finally, after all the "holds" and groans, up Glenn went, up until he was a pale white flame that popped (the room gasped) as he was finally freed from gravity and life and time as we knew it. Yet even then, I kept looking behind me, back at all those kids suffering this glorious national neck sprain, heads rocked back in awe at a rocket that, like life or model years, seemed it could only roar on forever, higher and faster, bigger and better, newer and newer still. Truly, it seemed that America had catapulted Happiness itself into orbit.

Then something happened—something I'd actually forgotten until several weeks ago. Where do they come from, those brain bubbles that slip out of nowhere, then flare like a match with a hot, sulfurous whiff of something? What popped into my mind was a chameleon, my little green chameleon Green Guy.

I was almost twelve and I'd bought Green Guy at the circus when it came to Washington, as it did then, and still does, every Easter. I'd gone there with the Carls down the street, a kindly older couple whose only child, Johnny, four or five years my junior, idolized me—idolized me in a way that, frankly, was as pathetic and embarrassing as the very reason the Carls had invited me. You see, a few months before this, my mom had died—died in spite of all the wonder drugs and specialists and, of all things, from an appendix, probably the piddliest, most useless piece of gut in the whole human body. Anyhow, with her gone, it was just my dad and me now. Which on our be-fruitful-and-multiply Catholic street didn't even count as a family. Shoot, on our street, they didn't have families, they had whole teams who piled into battered, tail-dragging station wagons, thudding off to mass or practice or whatever it was real families did.

Fine. So maybe our family had blown up on the launch pad, but *I* wasn't gonna feel sorry for me. So while I breathlessly watched from my bed, high above me in the darkness, suspended from the threads that held my model rockets, Green Guy hung—literally—by one spindly, green toe. It was all part of his astronaut training, while I, down in Mission Control, timed him with my luminous Timex watch.

Still, it was scalding. Humilating, really, how Green Guy would just take it, his long-tailed body twisted in that frozen, almost hiber-nating way in which reptiles endure torture. Boy, was he brave, though. One of our nation's best. Giving speeches in my head, al-most praying, I told him he was a very great man, good and strong and powerful, and that our whole country was depending on him. The guy was making real progress, too, progress not only in suspen-sion and centrifuge but in his greatest ordeal—underwater training.

Amazing thing. Even under water in the stoppered sink, Green Guy kept his eyes open, wide open with those filmy skin goggles which I figured lizards had developed to snorkel through the slime eons. I sure understood. Because, in the space of months, my eyes had peeled their own new skin, this to protect against the fierce wind and speed of what I myself was seeing just then. Which explains why we both understood each other, Green Guy and me, understood to the point that Green Guy would just stare up at me from the bottom, like he was croaking in his gargly, lizardy tongue, *roger*. Because Green Guy didn't beg life or people—no. Until the end, he didn't struggle, I guess to conserve air, but still it was awful for me, the steely concentration it took, having to hold him down until both our lungs were on fire—down until he'd start lashing around like he was in a dying monster movie and I'd have to yank his lizard butt out.

It was nip and tuck then. We gasped and trembled. We both got the bends. Huffing and freezing myself, blowing on him, I sat on the toilet, half crying for joy when I finally coaxed him back to life, and it was so eerily beautiful. Truly, it was like the first discovery of life, and I was its inventor. But almost as soon as I apprehended it, life, wondrous as a balloon, a whispery, Godlike voice also told me I was too late. Way, way too late to ever save my mom.

As for the world, my wide-eyed telescope had turned into a micro-scope, a burning, objectifying magnifying glass in which belief had turned to suspicion, love to doubt, and innocence to anger and contempt.

Now increasingly, what absorbed me was not space and techno-logical progress but rather a dumbstruck, more unconscious study of people. *Human progress* might be the convenient, catch-all adult

term for this new proclivity, although even for an adult, this would
be laying it on a little thick. A strictly psychological view might attri-
bute this new pessimism and self-scrutiny to my mother's death, but
this too would be an oversimplification, I think. In any case, the episode kindled in me a new alertness to change and self-deceit, a nervous rawness that directed me in much the way a burn intuits the
smallest shifts of wind. And now the wind was changing.

My faith in life. My life in faith. In this crisis of incoherence,
everything I'd once known was now up for grabs. I wondered why
bad people could have good kids, and good people could have bad
kids. Why even frankly dull-minded people could have superbright
kids, and schmoes insanely ambitious kids. Similarly, I wondered
why people said the things they did, and indeed if people, for all their
holier-than-thouing, ever got one iota better as people. Above all, I
smarted at the obvious lies people told themselves, adults and kids,
but grown-ups especially—adults like my father believing, against
all reason, in doctors in the first place and heaven in the second, and
worse when my mom was just as dead.

But mainly there was faith itching me like cotton wool, and all
the more when my own faith was dying. Still, living in our Catholic
fishbowl, such doubts were perilous—one because faith awed me,
and two because the so-called clean life yielded no clear outcome, or
at least none that I could see. I mean, how was it that folks like the
Portieres could be deeply religious, raise great kids, and survive almost anything, while the Harrolways—no less religious—seemed
to all die at the stake, producing nothing but dreary misfits and
hoodlums? It made no sense. None whatsoever.

Still, I do remember a kind of breakthrough during this confused
family-science period. It came when a kid handed me a mason jar
teeming with black tadpoles swimming in what looked like tobacco
spit. Well, I stopped dead. I goggled, then held it up to the sun, trans-
fixed not by the tadpoles but by the swirling silt, the almost volcanic
explosions of slime and goo. What absorbed me, though, wasn't the
science but rather what it seemed to explain about people—the almost cosmic joke or progress story of why the glittery, goldy particles
flew up even as the others sunk like lead, attracted as if by justice to

the muck on the bottom. Obviously, I'm not claiming I understood this in such patently allegorical adult terms—clearly, I didn't. Still, there was, I think, a reason why it consoled me as it did, why it cleared my mental lungs by at least objectifying a gnawing life problem.

Had I lived in the age of knee breeches and square-buckled shoes, I might have declared it proof of predestination. But living in my time, the rocket, having reversed course with my mother's death, was now wildly spinning. Dimly perhaps, I even knew the name for it. Chaos.

Today, after years of psychotherapy and sixteen years of mostly happy marriage, after good health, two wonderful children, money, and even some measure of worldly success, I see at bottom that I still feel this way, both about human progress and the technological and material progress that Americans commonly conflate into the same thing. I feel this way and it fills me with shame at my stubbornness, makes me feel unsound, nihilistic, and fundamentally unwise, and all the more at forty-six, when I know life is short, just as I know life is capable of moments of thrilling power, coherence, and beauty.

My religious faith died with my mother but obviously not the longing for coherence, that sense of life having a plan and a shape, a faith not in the final step but in the sure *next* step. This is, I think, what we really mean, consciously or not, when we even utter this quaint, now Pollyannish word *progress*. To me, it also helps explain the lemming pull of life today, when so many people seem to be desperately giving themselves over to "God"—to anyone or anything, crystals, witches, cults, fad diets. In turn, this desperation suggests the coeval pull of the religious Right and their own fantasy return to the 1950s, that never-never land before sex and drugs, Woodstock and Vietnam.

Still, whatever your particular remedies, it's obvious that a great many people, myself included, are looking for something clearly absent in the world we now inhabit. Against our time, the world I knew as a child is now so foreign that it requires an almost fictive effort to summon it: that dream of people shoulder to shoulder in church, praying in all sincerity for the president during the dark days of the bomb, that barn-heat of perspiring people singing in unison as the heaving pipe organ hollowed through my bones. Illusory or not, romantically or not, childishly or not, I recall in my lifetime a ringing certainty and direction that I'm quite certain I'll never see again. Nor will my children, I'm afraid.

Two or three times a year now—invariably, at my wife's or daughters' urging—we all go to a Unitarian church. Yet while I can attend and appreciate and even count my blessings (something I would have sneered at in my youth), I cannot sing, or certainly not in that rousing, unconscious way that truly parts life's darker waves. Meanwhile, for all my general mistrust of technogical progress, I'm hardly a Luddite. I don't bicycle to work, I consume as much as most Americans, and like most folks, I'm fascinated by science and gadgetry, even as the two blur in the public mind. I'm still dumbfounded that, with my cell phone, I can call home from the Mojave Desert or, with a few clicks of the mouse, show my daughters fresh images from Mars. For that matter, without the progress of in vitro fertilization, I know I wouldn't even have biological children, just as without the p.c. I might still be typing my first novel.

Still, even to entertain the word *progress,* I almost wince at what now seems a joke—a sucker's term. Significantly, though, I almost never hear the word, and then certainly not in the hopeful, unselfconscious way our parents might have used it. Like the buggy whip or ice-cream social, that vast dream of progress—big Progress, if you will—is a piece of Americana that has largely fallen into desuetude, a word with no real referent and thus no harbor in general speech.

This time, however, I don't think it's just me feeling sick in the back of the church. Nor am I alone when, like most New Age hypocrites, I speak out of both sides of my mouth, enjoying the fruits of technological and material progress, even as I high-mindedly shake my head at what it has wrought in a social sense, from environmental wreckage to celebrity worship to the continuing meltdown of public education and family. If anything, these two forms of progress seem wholly incompatible, like matter and antimatter, and this by sheer force of technology, which grinds everything into products, and products into junk. Microchips or celebrities, ideas or books: these are just effluvia fired into the afterburner of a hyperculture that lives, like a shark, by dint of sheer motion and, increasingly, for no reason *but* motion.

As I look back, it's clear that my parents—both raised poor—were themselves products of that postwar explosion of American progress. The GI-Bill education and VA home loan, the barbecue and two-week vacation—without being aware of it then, millions of Americans like my parents were in basic training, all learning to be prosperously middle class. To consume. To enjoy. Not to worry so much about money, although as Depression kids, my parents embodied the twin demons of prosperity, my dad saying "save" even as my mom said "spend."

My parents also embodied a powerful history—as did countless others who were that much closer to the wars, the boats, the camps, the chains, the shtetls and tenements, or simply the immigrant struggle to move up. Similarly, my parents' religion, such as it was, held a still mostly unbroken continuity with the past, a bond that you rarely see in today's born-again, twelve-step, know-nothing, make-your-own-sundae-style religions. Why, even Catholicism seems to have turned into a take-what-you-will-and-ignore-the-rest proposition, and who knows, maybe that's a healthy thing. For a writer like me, the telling thing here is my unusual ambivalence in even pronouncing on such moral matters. Honestly, as a man, I don't know what's right at this point, and perhaps this is the faith and consolation of writing fiction, a chance to tease from chaos a shape and from that shape the corresponding belief in a community that shares certain bedrock human assumptions about culture, value, and expression. In other words, if I want such a world, it increasingly seems that I must make it up.

But what on earth are we to do with the rapidly deteriorating conditions of ordinary life? Specifically, what are we to do as parents struggling to raise children in the odd chaos and anomie of our time? The paradox, it seems to me, is how sheltered many middle-class children are and also how miserably exposed, living in a world in which the bizarre occurs with ever more unremarkable frequency. Drug-crazed killings. Space suicide cults. The so-called Prom Mom who, at her high school prom, gave birth in the stall of the ladies' room, killed the baby, cleaned herself up, fixed herself a plate of food, then asked the band to play Metallica's "Unforgiven." Today, in tabloid America where every craziness has its chat room, even our urban myths are dying, and all for the appalling reason that all is thinkable and virtualizable, and hence almost instantly true.

In the meantime, like most parents, I experience periodic shocks at what life must be like for kids nowadays. Quietly depressing things, as when my eight-year-old daughter blithely asks, "Daddy, when you were a little boy, did your parents ever allow you to go out all by yourself? On your bike? Like to buy your own candy and see your friends?"

As if she's telling herself a fairy tale, my daughter fantasizes about freedom, that faraway land where she could ride her bike and buy candy, with the wind in her hair. Imagine: that freedom from fear which, from the day she was born, has kept her under eye, her and an entire generation. No wonder that today's best-parented children seem like flocks of sheep, sheep who can only assume that parents or care providers—the whole retinue of tutors, tenders, electronic paps, zaps, and nano-pets—are here to coddle them twenty-four hours a day. Sure, it's too much, but so is the fear of seeing your kid's face on the back of a milk carton. The terrible irony of my supposedly rebellious generation is that we're creating a herd of conformists. Precisely the kind of people we promised ourselves we'd never be.

At the same time, like our old dreams of progress, we ourselves have retreated into the woodwork. Cashed out, chilled out, burned out, we focus in despair or disgust on perhaps the only thing we *can* control or improve at this point—our children. As a result, we have turned our children into weirdly devotional objects. Little shrines to the faith we lost and the ideals we once held. Living protests against the public discourse we tune out and the elected officials we revile, against the employers we no longer trust and the work we secretly don't value. Against these blows, our kids are our last chance at redemption, with lives more structured, scheduled, coddled, and protected, more filled with lessons and mind-numbing self-improvement, than even our straitlaced forebears knew in the days of Sunday schools and family parlors.

Which brings me back to the Green Guy, my homunculoid hero and champion. Green Guy, my last green dream of childhood, suspended in the darkness while my own faith hung by a thread.

You already know the end of the story. Of course Green Guy fell one night and scurried under the molding—vanished into the cracks, just as I grew up and got on. All I can say is that, in my lifetime, I saw that space shot. I was an actual witness. In flame and smoke and thunder, I saw Progress fired at the heavens. I watched the whole thing go up, just as with my own eyes I saw it jettisoned, a spent booster rocket sacrificed to the speeding roar of the future and the emptier roar that now fuels it.

ALAN LIGHTMAN

Progress and the Individual

Over the last half-dozen years, friends and colleagues have become increasingly irritated at me for not being on the electronic network. Secretaries for distant committees call up and hound me for my electronic address, then lapse into stunned silence and confusion when they find that I don't have one. University administrators, who nowadays organize meetings and send messages across campus at the push of a button, grumble about hand-carrying information to me or putting paper in an envelope and sending it through the mail. I admit, I'm a nuisance. But I resist getting on e-mail as a matter of principle, as a last holdout against unbridled technology, galloping almost blind into the twenty-first century.

Let me give a few examples: An attorney recently wrote to me that her mental capacity to receive, synthesize, and appropriately complete a legal document has been "outpaced by technology." With the advent of the fax machine, overnight mail, and electronic mail, her clients want immediate turnaround, even on complex matters. She has consented, to please her customers, and the practice of law has, in her words, "forever changed from a reasoning profession to a marathon." A few days ago I was sitting at a seafood restaurant having lunch, when I looked over to the next table and spotted a woman doing business on her cellular phone while eating. At a recent birthday party for a friend's daughter, the father of the birthday child decided to record the event for posterity on his new video camera. Something malfunctioned with the equipment and he spent the entire time wrestling with the battery connections while the birthday event passed unseen before his eyes. Every summer, some friends rent a house in Maine for two weeks of vacation. They take along a fax machine, which they install on the kitchen counter next to the refrigerator, and a laptop computer with modem, which resides on a coffee table in the living room. The upscale retail company Hammacher Schlemmer has in its latest catalogue an advertisement for a correct-posture dog feeder for $44.95. In recent months, I've seen other companies advertise computer-controlled dog and cat feeders that open up at only preset times of the day, and remote-controlled mice for one's cat. Do any of these examples sound familiar?

For at least the last two hundred years, human society has operated under the unquestioned assumption that all developments in science and technology constitute progress. According to this view, if a new metal alloy can increase the transmission of data from ten million bits per second to twenty, then we should create it. If a new plastic has twice the strength-to-weight ratio as the older variety, we should produce it. If a new automobile can accelerate at twice the rate, we should build it. Whatever is technologically possible will find application and improve us.

The ordained imperative of advancing technology was probably thrust on its course at the start of the Industrial Revolution, although the idea must have had some velocity before then. As everyone knows, new technology in the eighteenth century, such as the power loom and the steam engine, dramatically improved the efficiency of production, and the associated financial rewards. Power looms enabled textile workers to perform at ten or more times their previous rate; furthermore, the machines never grew tired. Steam engines could produce up to one hundred times the power per weight as humans and oxen, and transformed England into an industrial and economic giant. With such outcomes, it was natural to equate technology with progress.

But that equation expressed far more than the obvious connection between technology and material improvement. The concept of progress became a major intellectual and cultural theme of the last century, fueled not only by the Industrial Revolution but also by the new theory of evolution. Many scientists and nonscientists of that period (and some today) interpreted biological evolution as a kind of progress from lower forms to higher, culminating in human beings. In the resulting view of progress, natural (biological) and human-made (technological) forces were together causing society to become more developed, organized, and moral with time. Progress became part of our manifest destiny. Writers, philosophers, and social thinkers, as well as scientists and engineers, took up these more general ideas. In England, the highly influential sociologist and philosopher Herbert Spencer attempted to synthesize the physical and social sciences and argued that a fundamental law of matter, "the persistence of force," inevitably brought about complexity, evolution, and progress in all things, cosmic and human alike. In America, Edward Bellamy's famous utopian novel *Looking Backward* (1888) described an optimistic view of the future in which labor problems have been solved by an "industrial army," efficient technology performs all unpleasant tasks and allows people to retire at age forty-five, and socialized medicine bestows long and healthy lives.

In the mid-nineteenth century, technology and our perception of it began to change. First, technology evolved from the individual-oriented "mechanical arts" (the word *technology* was not used before about 1880) like glassblowing and woodworking, to large, depersonalized technological systems, like the railroad. Each railroad required thousands of workers, tracks laid for hundreds or thousands of miles, many stations, and layers of bureaucracy and management. Each electric lighting system required generators, transmission lines, regulatory bodies, and so forth. These were the systems that occupied such men as Thomas Edison, Frederick Taylor, and Henry Ford. Edison, a transitional figure in the history of technology, was not only the private inventor and experimenter, but also the builder of the central electric station in New York City and the Edison General Electric plant in Schenectady, with its stables of engineers, managers, and financiers.

Secondly, at the same time as it got bigger, technology became an end in itself. Progress, which had once meant improvement in the human condition, with technology a means to that end, became equated directly with technology. Progress was technology. Technology was progress. Technology was the future. And finally, of course, the large technological systems, like the railroad, were opportunities for individuals to become rich to an unprecedented degree. The railroads were built by entrepreneurial businessmen like Cornelius Vanderbilt and John Pierpont Morgan, creating enormous fortunes for them. One knows who their counterparts are today.

Today, at the end of the twentieth century, a crucial question before us is whether developments in technology inevitably improve the quality of life. And, if not, how does our society employ some selectivity and restraint, given the enormous capitalistic forces at work? This is a terribly difficult problem for several reasons, not the least of which is the subjective nature of "progress" and "quality of life." Technology, by itself, does not possess values; the assessment of human progress requires them. We should not accept previous definitions of progress. Is progress greater human happiness? Greater comfort? Greater speed in personal transportation and communication? The reduction of human suffering? Longer life span? Even with a definition of progress, its measurements and technological requirements are not straightforward. If progress is human happiness, has anyone shown that twentieth-century people are happier than nineteenth-century people? If progress is comfort, what about the short-term comfort of air-conditioning systems versus the long-term comfort of a pollution-free environment? If progress is longer life span, should we continue to develop new medical technology to sustain terminally ill patients as long as possible?

Only a fool would claim that new technology rarely improves the quality of life. The electric light has expanded innumerable human activities, from reading to nighttime athletic events. Advances in medicine (particularly the germ theory of disease) public health programs, and the development of good antiseptics have clearly reduced physical suffering and substantially extended the healthy human life span.

I am not in favor of squashing new developments in pure science, in any form. The act of understanding the workings of nature, and our place in it, expresses for me what is most noble and good in us. As for the applications of science and the often imaginative creations of technology, I definitely support technology as a whole, and I benefit greatly from much of it. But we cannot have technology without an accompanying consideration of human values and the quality of life. For too long, we have simply assumed that every new gadget or technique or increase in speed represents progress.

How should this examination and questioning proceed? It is not likely that government regulations would be effective. Our government, as well as other large institutions, understandably have an investment in allowing technology to develop unabated. Regulation of technology seems questionable on other grounds as well. Such people as Anthony Lovins and E. F. Schumacher have argued for "appropriate" technologies like windmills, local energy sources, small and efficient machines. These ideas have value, but they cannot be regulated from the top for the same reason that we cannot regulate the books published each year. American writers and publishers currently present the public with 50,000 books a year, not all of them of high merit. But any type of regulation would inevitably eliminate good books as well as bad. Decisions about what books are worthwhile are best left to the individual reader.

If we are to take individual responsibility for our relationship to technology, we cannot be passive consumers. The consumer must better understand his or her self-interest. This understanding, in turn, requires an understanding of the true cost of a piece of technology. And here, ultimately, may lie the critical issue. What is the true cost of technology and consumption, and how do we measure it? We understand the gain very well. But what is the cost? Thoreau framed the question so well: "If it is asserted that civilization is a real advance in the condition of man . . . it must be shown that it has produced better dwellings without making them more costly; and the cost of a thing is the amount of what I will call life which is required to be exchanged for it, immediately or in the long run." Somehow, we must figure out how to measure the life exchanged for each piece of technology, and we must balance that life against our actual needs, physical and mental. This accounting may have to be done item by item, hour by hour, but it can be done only by the individual. Only the individual can measure his own spirit and life. Today's technology overload is a national malaise, but it is also a deeply personal malaise. The responsibility for combating the illness does not lie with the system. It lies with the individual.

BILL McKIBBEN

The Problem with
Wildlife Photography

There's a bright blue sky in the woods this morning, sun lifting from behind the mountain, snow mostly melted but ice still scabbed on the northward slopes. What living things do I see? Only a red-winged blackbird, and a startled blur of quail whirring off through the branches. And several piles of scat—deer, hare, coon, coyote.

This essay, ostensibly a brief study of certain controversies about wildlife photography, raises an unlikely question: in the time now approaching—inarguably an age of limits—will we want to find limits for ideas and expressions as we will for things?

The art of wildlife photography employs quite a few people scattered around the country. Filmmakers supply hour upon hour of video for PBS, the major networks, and cable channels. Still photographers take pictures for magazines, calendars, books, and advertisements, and they market countless trips for amateurs and aspiring professionals, teaching them the tricks of the trade. And their images do a lot of good—from Flipper and Jacques Cousteau to the mountain lion nuzzling her kit on your latest mailing from an environmental group, they've helped change how we see the wild. I've seen neighbors of mine, who had no use for wolves, begin to melt during a slide show about the creatures. It is no great exaggeration to say that dolphin-safe tuna flows directly from the barrel of a Canon, that without Kodak there'd be no Endangered Species Act.

At the same time, and in more easily observable ways than with other kinds of art, wildlife photography raises ethical problems. They stem from the fact that most animals are extremely shy and extremely good at keeping their distance from people. I walk in the woods every day here, and mostly it's like this morning's trek—the occasional sign of wildlife, but very rarely the sight, especially of those charismatic fauna most highly prized by magazine editors and calendar makers. I see raccoons pretty often, but I've come across bears twice in all my years in the Adirondacks, and that's twice more than most of my neighbors. I once spent several days in a bug-ridden North Carolina swamp helping researchers from the Fish and Wildlife Service try to trap a few red wolves. These wolves were wearing radio collars and we had the receiver, and we still managed not even a glimpse—just the occasional scatter of feathers or fur where they'd made a meal.

In a partial effort to overcome this handicap, wildlife photographers, who include among their number some of the most accomplished and intrepid outdoorspeople I know, have copied a number of strategies from hunters. Filmmakers, for whom the rewards are greatest and the costs of waiting around the highest, have been accused of staging scenes—the *Denver Post,* in a recent series, quoted employees of the PBS series *Wild America* as saying animals had been tied to posts with fishing line so that others could attack them, a charge the program's host denies. Still photographers may wait by a water hole for animals to come in and drink; they may spread a little bait (bears like jelly doughnuts); they may lure in animals with decoys or with calls. All of those strategies cause problems, of course. An animal may smell someone hiding in a blind by a water hole and steer clear, though he needs the water. A wolf might have been hunting fruitlessly for three days, near the end of her strength, when she chases off after a tape recording of a baby rabbit. I've talked to a photographer who scared a cougar off a mountain goat it killed; the result was that it had to kill another goat. And even these strategies don't always work, especially with the shiest creatures. "I don't know of any pros who have gotten pictures of cougars without going to the extreme of tracking them down with dogs and treeing them," says Art Wolfe, one of the country's premier wildlife photographers. Erwin Bauer, a veteran of the profession, owns a hundred acres in Montana. "From time to time a mountain lion comes through. I know he does, because I see his tracks, find deer he's killed. But we never see the animal."

To overcome such problems, wildlife photographers have increasingly turned in recent years to a series of private game farms, small zoos. Jay Diest runs the Triple D Game Farm in Kalispell, Montana. It is home to a long list of "primary species" (black bear, wolf, lynx, bobcat, cougar, mountain lion, arctic fox, fisher, wolverine, river otter) as well as a number of "secondary species" (badger, raccoon, porcupine, mink, snowshoe hare, and wild turkey). Still photographers pay three hundred dollars a day to stand outside the "professionally designed enclosures" and shoot one primary species; if you want to shoot three primary species, the fee drops to two hundred dollars apiece. But the grizzly bear cub—he's four hundred dollars. "They respond to certain commands," says Diest. "They will stand up, they will sit, they will pretend like they're growling. On command they will get up on things—if you want them up on a large rock, they will get up there. They will strike poses." The animals are by all accounts well fed and humanely treated, and they have an increasing number of peers in other places. Montana alone now boasts three such operations, and tropical countries as well are getting into the act. There is, for instance, a famously approachable jaguar in a game farm in Belize that several picture editors told me about—if you've seen a photo of a jaguar recently, there's a good chance it's this one.

Pictures taken at game farms are not uncommon. One day a couple of years ago, for instance, the staff at *Natural History* gathered to plan a piece on cougars. The photo editor projected slide after slide on the walls, remembers managing editor Ellen Goldensohn. "She told us to guess which ones were captive animals and which were wild. Most of the really good ones turned out to be from the game farms." If you see a close-up of a snake in a magazine, it almost certainly hasn't been taken in the wild, but instead in a cage designed by a herpetologist and outfitted with lights. "In the field, copperheads are quite rarely seen in a noncluttered environment," says photographer Joe MacDonald. "They live in brush piles—you're never going to see them from a ground-level perspective. You're not belly to belly with them." It's not just still photos, either—a great many of the television nature sequences come straight from the game farms. Such images—I repeat—can be easily defended, both as more ethical than those shot in the wild and as necessary for a greater good. "Game farm animals are like animal soldiers," says MacDonald. "In a war you have people who die to save democracy. These animals, which are not suffering, are also playing a very important role. Without the pretty pictures, would there be the same affection for them?"

But there are problems here, too, severe ones. You get a small hint of them when you talk to wildlife biologists like Don White at Montana State University. "I'll see a picture and say, 'How in the world did he get that? It's got to be staged. But it's passed on as part of the natural world.' And then you understand when you see an elderly lady bail out of her car and run up to a grizzly to take a picture. She got within fifteen feet. Fortunately he didn't think she was important enough to kill. But it's that kind of thing that makes you wonder if we're communicating any kind of common-sense understanding of animals." That elderly lady was not alone. Chuck Bartlebaugh, director of the Center for Wildlife Information, spends much of his time trying to reduce encounters between Yellowstone tourists and Yellowstone bears, who end up being shot when they become too habituated to tourists. After surveying four hundred people who were taking pictures along the roads, he and his colleagues concluded that the images provided by professional nature photographers were the biggest cause of problems. "We asked these people where they got their information that it was safe to approach bears or elk or whatever, and they immediately referred to TV programs and other pictures that showed biologists or photographers getting close to animals. A lot of the magnificent shots that the public tries to imitate in our national parks were taken of captive animals with handlers there." Chuck Jonkel, who runs the International Wildlife Film Festival, instructs his judges to scrutinize pictures carefully. "Some of those pictures tell a lie. They say you can get this close to an animal."

Wildlife photographers and editors, to their credit, have begun to think seriously about the peril that game farm photos might pose both to hapless shutterbugs and to our general understanding of the natural world. And the solution slowly gaining ground is to label photos, either in the caption or the photo credit, as coming from game farms. Videomaker Marty Stouffer, whose *Wild America* series for public television has come under particular attack, has offered to label "factual recreations" in his footage. Some photographers say such fine print is entirely unnecessary; others that they might favor it when sending pictures to a scientific publication like *Natural History* but not to an advertising agency; others simply label their slides and let editors decide. It's akin to the warning labels on cigarettes, even closer to the warnings that carmakers flash on the screen before a commercial showing the latest model careening down both lanes of some mountainous highway. That it probably won't matter very much can be assumed from the photographer's credo about the relative worth of a picture and a thousand words.

But even if it did reduce the number of Kodachrome maulings, little labels on a picture can't overcome the deepest problems, which have to do with how we perceive the world, in this case, the natural world. After a lifetime of nature shows and magazine photos, we arrive at the woods conditioned to expect splendor—surprised when the parking lot does not contain a snarl of animals attractively mating and killing each other. Because all we get is close-ups, we've lost much of our sense of how the world actually operates, of the calm and quotidian beauty of the natural world, of the fact that animals are usually preoccupied with hiding, or wandering around looking for food. There is something frankly pornographic about the animal horror videos ("Fangs!") marketed on late-night TV, and even about some of the shots you see in something as staid as *Natural History*. Here is an emerald boa eating a parrot—the odds, according to the photographers I talked to, were "jillions to one" that it was a wild shot. Indeed, the photographer who took it boasted to *People* magazine about how he'd spray-painted ferrets to convert them to the endangered blackfooted kind, and how he'd hoisted tame and declawed jaguars into tree branches for good shots, and starved piranhas so they'd attack with great ferocity. Another photographer took a game stab at defending the shot of the emerald boa munching down the parrot—"It very graphically illustrates the relationship between higher and lower vertebrates," he said. So it does—but that's a little like saying Miss September graphically illustrates the development of the mammary gland in *Homo sapiens*.

Even worse, perhaps, is the way the constant flow of images undercuts the sense that there's actually something wrong with the world. How can there really be a shortage of whooping cranes when you've seen a thousand images of them—seen ten times more images than there are actually whooping cranes left in the wild? In Ellen Goldensohn's words, "They imply an Edenic world. And yet the real world is shrinking cruelly." No one ever shows a photograph of the empty trees where there are no baboons anymore; whatever few baboons remain are dutifully pursued until they're captured on film, and even if all the captions are about their horrid plight, the essential message of the picture remains: baboons.

At this point we could—indeed we should—start talking about a new ethic. People have tried, from time to time, to promulgate ethics for most of the arts, and nature photography is no exception. As the photographer Daniel Dancer points out in a recent issue of *Wild Earth* magazine, the British organization of nature photographers issues a single commandment: "The welfare of the subject is more important than the photograph." It's an apt rule, but as Dancer also points out it does nothing to address the larger questions I've alluded to, what he calls "the impact on society and our relationship to nature as a *whole*. If overimaging the world furthers our separation from nature, then there is something inherently wrong in our covenant with the camera." He offers a number of practical ways that individual photographers might rewrite that covenant—by offering "sacrifices" to their "prey" by using the photos for advocacy purposes, for instance, and by shooting the clear-cut next to the forest, too.

Others offer suggestions from the point of view of an editor. Fred Ritchin, for instance, former picture editor of the *New York Times* magazine and author of *In Our Own Image: The Coming Revolution of Photography* calls much of nature photography "nostalgia at this point—and a vicious kind of nostalgia, like big game hunters putting the horns of an elephant over their fireplace." Instead of worrying about game farms, he says editors could rethink their whole approach. "I might want to send a photographer out to spend a week with a snake and take notes and photograph the snake every hour for the entire time. Or to begin to take pictures of what the photographer understands would be the point of view of the snake. Or photograph snake fragments for a week, as if it were a disembodied thing. So you could really see it, as opposed to saying, 'There's only one part of a snake that's interesting—it's head—and only one or two poses, and we're going to do them over and over again.'"

Reading and talking to such thinkers, though, it's easy to find a note of resignation—the deep suspicion that such rhetoric is not going to affect very quickly or very profoundly the marketplace in which photographers operate. If one photographer or editor falters, chances are there will be another to take his place, offering the nostrils of the snake. Changing course even slightly makes an editor nervous, says Ritchin, because "you might not be pleasing your readership. It's like going out on your first date. Once you've told a great joke you don't want to tell a more matter-of-fact joke." Dancer offers the wise advice of Wendell Berry that "one must begin in one's own life the private solutions that can only in turn become public solutions." That is so. But my work on environmental issues has made me wary of completely private solutions—the momentum of our various tragedies makes the slow conversion of small parts of the society insufficient. Aren't we ethically impelled to also try to imagine ways that such private solutions might turn into public and widespread practice?

And it's precisely for that reason that wildlife photography interests me so much. It's a small enough world that, at least for purposes of argument, you could postulate real changes. Suppose the eight or nine magazines that run most of the nature photos, and the three or four top TV nature shows, formed among them a cooperative or clearinghouse for wildlife pictures, and announced that anyone could mail them as many slides as they wished for their files by a certain date. *And that after that date they wouldn't take any new submissions.* Then, when the editors of *Natural History* decided they needed some elephant photos, the staff of the cooperative agency could send them a wide array to choose from. For the fact is, there are already plenty of elephant photos in the world—when *Wildlife Conservation* was planning a piece on elephants a few years ago, according to art director Julie Maher, they reviewed ten thousand slides. If *Nova* needed a mountain lion, they could ask for the miles of film already shot and then make their selections.

If some member of the consortium had a good reason for needing a new picture—if there was a new species, or a new behavior that needed illustrating, or someone was needed to accompany a scientific expedition—then the cooperative could assign a photographer, along with strict instructions about conduct; about how far away to stay, for instance. These measures might solve some of the ethical problems involving treatment of animals. And it's possible such an agency could also eventually begin to deal with the larger questions, too—for instance, over time, it could cull from its stock extreme close-ups and other kinds of photos that miseducate viewers about the natural world. It's the kind of place where a new ethic might *adhere,* might grow into something powerful.

Since most of the competitors would belong to this cooperative, the commercial pressure that prevents such backing-off at the moment might diminish; no one else would have a two-inch-away close-up of the golden tamarind monkey either. "A big problem we see is an editor who says 'I want this kind of picture,' and then the word gets out," says Chuck Jonkel of the Wildlife Film Festival. "They'll say, 'Give us a picture of a caribou running full tilt and we'll give you $1,700.' Someone's going to hire a helicopter and run the shit out of them so they can get their $1,700. I don't blame the photographer for that—I blame the editors." Such pressure would ease; there'd be a place to bring complaints. At the same time, such an agency could become a real center for those who wanted to use cameras to document the ongoing destruction of animals and habitat that is the crucial chore for nature journalists in the late twentieth century.

It is not even completely quixotic to imagine such a clearinghouse forming, I think. Most of the magazines involved are the publications of various environmental groups or nonprofit societies like the National Geographic; a good deal of the film appears on public channels here and abroad. A fairly small number of members of these groups might become convinced that these issues are important and campaign for the formation of such an agency, which would have the added benefit of saving money for the participating enterprises; once it was well established, no serious publication could afford to operate without its seal of approval. (Check out your supermarket and see how much non-dolphin-safe tuna they're selling.) There would surely be all sorts of advertisers and calendar makers and rogue video artists—but at least there'd be something to measure them against.

Imagining institutions allows you to test the strength of the ethic on which they're based against very real and practical objections. In this case, the most obvious drawback is that it would put photographers out of work, or force them to find new subjects. If it worked as planned, this cooperative agency would need very few new wildlife photos annually—no one would be paying for zebras anymore. And this, we intuitively feel, is not fair—who am I, or you, to tell someone else how they can or can't make a living. We're reasonably comfortable with the process as long as the impersonal economy makes the decision. We don't grieve for blacksmiths, and the tears we shed over the "downsized" are, frankly, few. If public fashion changed suddenly and there was no *demand* for photos of animals, no one would suggest supporting photographers in their vocation. But it feels different to set out on a campaign that would as a direct byproduct put people out of work. Still, it's not much different from, say, enacting zoning laws in a town—you can be pretty certain that'll cut the work for carpenters. Or say you campaign for a recycling system in your community—it's only a matter of time before some mill-worker in Maine loses his job.

In this case, though, you couldn't even argue that new work will be created. Newspaper recycling, after all, creates whole new categories of occupation—collecting the papers, working in sorting plants, running recycling mills. This potential clearinghouse for wildlife photos would announce, in effect: We've got enough images now; we can recycle them more or less forever; please don't bother taking any more. And since negatives don't really degrade with use, that would be that. *It is an almost unknown thing in our society to say, "That's enough."* To answer the question "How much is enough" with "We've got plenty."

And it sounds especially heretical in any creative endeavor. The word *censorship* rises unbidden to one's lips. And even if you can convince yourself that it's not really censorship—it's not the government, after all; it's no more censorship than some magazine telling you they won't print your story for whatever damn reason; it's *editing*—even so, it seems repressive. It *is* repressive. It's the imposition of a new taboo, something we've rarely done in recent centuries. We've been about the business of demolishing taboos, and we've succeeded. Consumers aren't supposed to have taboos; they're supposed to consume, and consume we do: not just goods and services, but images, ideas, knowledge. Nothing is off limits. So there's something a little creepy about saying, "We'll be buying no new photos of wildebeests. We don't think it's a good idea to be taking them." It is a new taboo—do we want any new taboos?

The case I've constructed about wildlife photography depends for its clarity on several peculiarities: the obvious problems (as well as benefits) inherent to the practice; the fact that it might conceivably be voluntarily restrained because of the size and the environmentally minded sponsorship of the industry; most crucially, perhaps, the fact that animals evolve very slowly and so there is little rationale for constantly redocumenting them. By contrast, pornography can obviously be destructive, but since *Hustler* isn't published by the National Organization for Women you'd need government involvement with all the dangers that portends. (Either that or you'd need a new taboo to spread among the consumers of pornography.) Documentary films or photos or writings about people can cause real problems for their subjects, which is one reason anthropologists have evolved codes for their work; but human societies evolve so quickly and radically that it's unlikely we'd ever reach the point where we would want to simply stop that kind of journalism. Still, a developing *sense* of taboo wouldn't hurt these endeavors—a sense that one was treading on somewhat sacred ground, and so needed to proceed with care.

I can remember writing a piece for *The New Yorker* on homelessness. I was twenty-one, had just moved to the city, and Mr. Shawn, the editor, asked me to spend some time living on the streets—this was before the idea had become cliché, before people had completely noticed homelessness as a crisis. And it was a good, absorbing piece. A few years later I reprised it—spent another fascinating stretch living without a roof. I spent time at the last remaining private flophouse in the city, and in the vast armory at 168th Street where thousands of men slept each night, and on the endless A train run to Rockaway, a mobile dormitory for dozens of men and women. And yet when the time came to run the piece, I pulled it at the last minute, out of some inchoate sense that this would hurt, not help; that it was part of what was by now a flood of media, the total impact of which was to normalize that crisis, to make it seem not a crisis at all but an inevitable fact of urban living, like pigeons.

As I've become more interested in environmental matters I've thought a lot about these questions of restraint, about when one's curiosity or creative impulse can be bane as well as boon. About whether there are places where taboos once more make sense. It's easier to see when it comes to things, not ideas. Clearly, for instance, we'd be better off environmentally if as a culture we frowned on automobiles; if we said that the freedom they afforded was not worth the cost in terms of global warming, suburban sprawl, and so forth. And a taboo against the next ever-larger version of the Ford Explorer, even if it somehow developed, wouldn't seem a real threat to the human spirit.

But there are other, tougher questions, ones that focus more clearly on ideas. Take genetic engineering as an example, the greatest creative endeavor now gripping the scientific community. There's probably more human imagination being spent on this task than on any other. And for good reason—it carries certain obvious hopes, like the eradication of childhood diseases. But it also carries certain great dangers, I think, and in the wake of Dolly the doppelgänger sheep, I am not alone in thinking so. It gives most people a slightly queasy feeling if they think about it, not so much because they fear the creation of some Frankenstein germ, but because they sense the implication for the human soul of seizing control of every force around us on the planet. Do we want to be redesigning the most basic biological instructions, inevitably for the benefit of our species? Perhaps we do—perhaps what we want most is a sort of shopping mall world, planned solely for our material ease and delight. Perhaps we don't. I'm not making the case for a new taboo here, one that might allow us to limit our tinkering to cystic fibrosis and muscular dystrophy. All I'm saying is that it's an open debate.

But it's a debate we're incapable of having because we operate under the assumption that debate is unnecessary, even repellent. We take as a given that we should find out everything we can, develop everything we can, photograph and write about everything we can, and then let the marketplace decide what to do with it. By definition, therefore, if it sells it is good. We've short-circuited the process of thinking things through as a culture—which may be the basic task of a culture. We have no way to entertain the possibility of restraint as a society—even mentioning that we might not want to find out everything there is to know about the genetic code seems deeply repressive.

And yet self-restraint is the uniquely human gift, the one talent no other creature or community possesses even as a possibility.

The sky by afternoon has turned shiny gray, but it's warm, and the woods are noisy—a crow caw-cawing nearby, angry about something I can't see. A blur of rabbit catches the corner of my eye. I nestle in the big root of a hemlock and watch a squirrel hop branches.

NOELLE OXENHANDLER

The Lost While

Once I happened to find myself sitting on the sandy bank of a New England pond with a famous Latin American novelist. We watched as a woman with thick wavy hair that went down to her waist entered the water.

"Look how thin and pale she is," he said. "You can see that her hair consumes all her life energy." Her hair floated out around her like a brown seal. He became more excited. "It's like an animal growing out of her head. . . ."

"Yes," I said. I felt I was witnessing an actual moment of magic realism. Then, as some children went into the water and began to paddle and splash, he grew melancholic. He was missing his nine-year-old daughter, who had stayed behind in Chile. He began to tell me about her. How beautiful she was. She had green eyes shaped like almonds and golden hair. Then he told me that he and his wife had adopted her as an infant. When she was five years old, they told her that she had been born to other parents.

"And do you know what she did?" he asked me. "She didn't cry. She didn't say a word. She went into our bedroom. She climbed onto our bed and she curled up at the foot of it. She lay there, in fetal position, for an entire afternoon."

I have always remembered this story. The sureness with which the child, her world upheaved, took care of herself. With a knowing as deep as whatever it is that prompts a cat, about to give birth, to find the inside of a drawer or a pile of hay, she knew she could not go forward without going back. She had to leave the linear movement of time and take her place inside a different rhythm: slow, circular, recursive.

We have all had such moments of true urgency. The morning before my daughter was born—though I didn't know that the birth would begin that night—I woke knowing I had to get to a body of water. The excursion was impractical and irrational, involving a drive along rough bumpy roads, miles away from the house or the hospital. For hours I lay like a beached whale, unable to get comfortable on my thin towel spread over sharp pebbles. But, for some reason I could not have put into words, I knew as I looked out at the expanse of clear blue lake that my being there was necessary.

Ne-ked-ti: no drawing back. There is a *no* at the root of necessity. True urgency involves a kind of winnowing. The wheat from the chaff. The *yes* from the *no*. The foot of the bed. The body of water. The narrowness of *this,* not that.

When the alarm clock rings, what sort of urgency is that? *Get up. Get up.* "It is we who invest the alarm clock with its urgency," Sartre said. But it is so difficult to grasp this. The metallic ring and the acid squirt of anxiety in the gut or throat seem so simultaneous as to preclude even an instant of recognition.

Why has it become so difficult, except in moments of extremis, to attend to an inner sense of necessity? Not long ago in upstate New York, I visited my friend Margaret. She is recovering from ten years of brutally intense political engagement with the world. In her new regime, she swims every day, she takes walks in the late evening light through her neighborhood, enjoying the patterns of shadow and streetlight and noticing the shapes of the trees. When we walk together, our progress is slow and I find her as ruthlessly present as a puppy or a small child. We have to keep stopping to pick up acorns, to smell the night jasmine, or to exclaim over the early color of a fallen leaf.

Yet frequently I have to repeat to her the words *brutal . . . recovery . . . the world*. As a friend, it seems I am required to be a kind of hypnotist, providing ballast against the fierce prevailing winds. Deep down she knows how desperately she needs an interval of restoration, but the conditioning is so powerful. On the wall of her study is a recent gift from her father, the now retired president of a large department store. A framed photograph of a magnificent wave bears, in huge letters, the caption "DO IT NOW!" The implication is clear: the perfect wave crests in one moment only, and then it is gone forever. The price of a pause is irrevocable loss.

I love the word *pause*. For me it is onomatopoetic: the way the double vowel opens slowly like the folds of an accordion, forcing us to drawl. We know that the photograph of the perfect wave emerged from countless hours: the photographer huddled in the sand, the prints developing in the dark in their chemical bath. The lion's share of any surfer's life is the getting up before dawn, the floating, paddling, dreaming, counting, "Not this one . . . not yet. . . ." But what goes up on the wall is the crest with its exhortation. Now or never.

The hardest thing, it seems, is to withdraw from the frantic sphere of activity, to trust the inner sense of urgency when it tells us: *lie low*. Once a week Margaret goes to the cake shop and buys cake-sized cardboard circles. When she comes home she puts music on and begins to draw on the circles. I have watched her. Her face is rapt, her body absorbed in the process of drawing. For years she's had to steel herself against the process of introspection, lest it leave her too raw and exposed to face the political fray. Now she is amazed at the images that emerge—among them, a recurring grove of pines. They startle her, almost as if they belonged to someone else. She has been famished for such a process of revelation, and gradually her room is filling with the chalk-and-cardboard mandalas.

Yet again and again, she describes the activity as "self-indulgent." Sometimes, to keep her from giving up, I have to remind her of all she has gone through: cancer caused by the drugs her pregnant mother was prescribed, ravaging surgery, years of bitter legal battling, medical lobbying before Congress, and—just on the heels of success—betrayals from within her closest ranks. But why should it take such a litany of suffering to justify a fallow time?

"Did I tell you about Jacques Lusseyran?" I asked Margaret the other day. In spite of being blinded at the age of eight, he was a member of the French Resistance and a survivor of Buchenwald. When I read his autobiography, what impressed me as much as his heroic activity was the pause that preceded it. For weeks, he simply absorbed the reality of Paris under the Occupation—a strange emptiness in the streets, except for certain neighborhoods that swarmed with Nazi soldiers. There he heard the rhythm of their speech, the sound of their boots, and smelled the unfamiliar odor of their tobacco. At last, following a bad bout of measles, he understood that he and a band of his schoolmates would come together in solidarity. Still, despite his acute sense of emergency, he felt there was something else he needed to do before throwing himself into the fire. Finally, it came to him: he would take dancing lessons. "I learned all the basic dance steps in two weeks," he writes,

> as fast as parched people quench their thirst in midsummer. I covered the whole range from waltz to swing and became a real fan of swing, not for aesthetic reasons as you may guess, but because swing was really a dance to drive out demons. When you had whirled a pack of girls at arm's length for five or six hours, with all their perfume coming back at you by the handful, you were dead beat. But still you had driven off the devils. And they are made to be shaken, these devils, whether they are political or individual.

What courage to dance on the brink of war, on the threshold of Buchenwald. To give oneself the time to evoke or to exorcise whatever inner forces were needed, or stood in the way of, action. And how difficult—except from hindsight—to see this as courage. Fiddling while Rome burns. An ostrich with its head in the sand. In the press of events, aren't *these* the images that arise for us? The alarm clock rings. The same voice that repeats "self-indulgent" describes the boy's dancing as whistling in the dark, an act of bravado.

At root, the words *courage* and *bravado* are worlds apart. Courage comes from *cor,* heart, from what is most interior. *Bravado,* and the related words *brave* and *bravery,* trace back to *barbary,* and refer to what is primitive, unrefined, uncivilized, un-Greek—foreign.

When the young girl goes to lie at the foot of the bed to be reborn, this time to her adoptive parents, she is taking the foreign—the primitive, brute fact that has come crashing in on her, *you were not born to us*—and mixing it with her own being. This is the *cor,* the movement of interiority, that is the heart of courage. It involves an attunement of inner and outer, the particular terms of which—dancing lessons, a long bumpy road to a lake, a trip to the cake store for cardboard circles—don't necessarily appear either rational or expedient.

"It still takes nine months to make a baby," an old French woman told me recently. She was shaking her head, in a wry, amused way, at the hubris of modern life, with its implied assumption and demand that processes be infinitely shortened, collapsed into themselves—until there is no such thing as process anymore, only a succession of maximally productive moments.

The green cash that emerges at the press of a button. The piece of paper in California that immediately yields a piece of paper in New York. Where does it end? With the letter that is read in the moment of its being conceived in the mind of the sender, with the bread that is eaten before it is baked.

This is magic time. God-time. When thinking, speaking, and doing are one. "Let there be light!" God said. And there was light. This is the ancient wish of the human being: to reside in the place where one need only to open one's mouth to make a world happen. As a child, when I woke up thirsty in the middle of the night and couldn't face the long walk down a cold hall to the sink, I would lie in my bed and open my mouth, imagining a shiny soda fountain in the sky that would release just the cold, flavored stream, minty or lime, I wished for. At times it became unbearable to lie there, with my dry mouth open, knowing that no matter how intensely I wished, not a single drop would fall from the sky. The fall from grace is the fall from simultaneity, exile from the garden where the fruit is at hand and to desire is to eat. Henceforth you will have to work for your food, and to give birth—to bring into being—will be difficult.

Suffering this curse, is it any wonder we take such delight in the *presto* of our own inventions? With each movement toward the instantaneous, we put a toe back in paradise, that place where to wish is to have. With each movement toward simultaneity, we are back, however fleetingly, in the womb, where we don't even need to wish in order to be warm, held, fed.

But here is the lawyer, riding the train between Tarrytown where he lives and New York City where he works. It's a beautiful ride, along the Hudson River, past the Tappan Zee Bridge and the high green cliffs of the Palisades. He could spend the early morning commute watching the slowly emerging sun break the dark river into moving strokes of gold and pink light. But all the while he is clicking, tapping, speaking to people who are somewhere else. For now it is possible to carry an office inside a briefcase: a laptop, a fax-modem, a phone. . . .

Convenience: the roots of the word are *with* and *come*. Everything can come with him now, onto the train. Every moment can be maximally productive. But what of the moment Yasunari Kawabata wrote of, in his novel *Snow Country?* An eye, looking through a darkened train window to the night outside, sees itself and then sees, inside itself, another eye, floating on the moving glass. Such a moment represents a kind of time that is vanishing: a floating time, completely free of usefulness, suspended between wakefulness and sleep, when the mind can be seized by the beautiful strangeness of life. An eye on a window. A woman's hair, floating around her like a brown seal. This is the time zone of wonder, when we fall out of the habitual, the taken-for-granted, and are startled by *what is*. It is a world away from the world of convenience, where everything is simply there, available, to be used as the means—laptop, fax-modem, phone—for our own preconceived ends.

Now there are trains that go so fast the eye can't even take in the landscape. Among the greatest pleasures in my life has been to sit on a French train, watching each village, with its steeple and stone walls, emerge in turn from the intervening pattern of field and trees and those beautiful cows—Charolais—that are the color of silt or of cream sinking into a cup of coffee. But now, on the TGV—those trains that can whip from Paris to Provence in a matter of four hours—the trees and the villages turn into a blinking pattern of stripes, bars that give me a headache and I have to look away. For the sake of speed, in the interest of not wasting time, we sacrifice the sensuous richness of the not-yet. If we put up with increasing discomfort in travel—the seats that grow more and more cramped, the air thinner, the food more vestigial on the ever more crowded airplanes—it's because the in-between time no longer fully exists for us in its own right.

"While-U-Wait," the signs say, because we are too rushed to bother with the silent *Y-o* of *You,* and because we cannot bear waiting that is not simultaneously productive. Just to sit under the bright lights of the Jiffy Lube waiting room, sipping coffee in a styrofoam cup and leafing through a magazine while my car's fluids are being drained and exchanged provides a rare sense of luxury. After all, I could be balancing my checkbook, grading my students' papers. . . . Even in the space of the While-U-Wait, I feel I should be doing something else, something more.

Yet some of my most pleasureable moments have come when I allowed myself to sink into the feeling that something was taking place without—or in the aftermath of—my conscious intervention. To sit in the sun, reading a book, while under a damp towel and the shade of my chair, a ball of bread dough rose in a bowl or six glass jars of hot milk thickened into yogurt. To lie on my back in the grass watching the clouds, my wet mop beside me, while inside the house the water-shapes dried on clean, lemony wood floors. The precious while that follows when you have done your part, and surrendered the work of your hands to powers as great as sun, air, time.

In the same way, I used to love the feeling of dropping a letter in the box. For several days, the letter-in-transit would hover around the edges of my consciousness. This delay was an intrinsic part of the pleasure of letter writing. It was a special tense all its own: when the "must do" turns into the "just done." And as the letter hovered, I also savored a kind of prescience in relation to my friend. During those two or three days I knew, at least in some small measure, what would befall her: *a letter in the box!* As Iris Murdoch has written, "The sending of a letter constitutes a magical grasp upon the future."

But now the old magic has given way to the new. One by one— save for a tiny handful of us who feel more and more self-consciously quaint—everyone I know has abandoned paper and ink in favor of more simultaneous modes of communication. And though a fax or an e-mail may lie in wait for their recipient, they nonetheless get from here to there in a matter of moments, and their waiting has none of the sealed mystery about it that attends a letter in its envelope.

In my professional writing life, too, I used to luxuriate in the feeling of sending an article off in the mail. There would be a few days' reprieve during which I could bask in the sense of a task accomplished. At the same time, I could attend to those aspects of my life that I'd been neglecting. Freed of the pressure of deadline, there was a certain voluptuousness in the most mundane chores: pulling the weeds in my garden, sorting through drawers, untangling the necklaces in my jewelry box. . . .

Increasingly, such simple and simply comforting chores feel like a form of indulgence. For now each writing cycle culminates in a frenzy of faxing, with a nearly instantaneous transmission of freshly completed manuscript, requests for revisions, revisions, more requests for revisions—and then a lapse back into silence, absence, a complete disconnection from which I feel compelled to launch a new round of activity. It is a rhythm I find jarring, an all-or-nothing, ON/OFF mode of being.

What we lose in this binary approach is the richness of the intermediate zone, the mysterious lushness of the latent, the almost, the not-yet. This is why, for some women, pregnancy is a uniquely redemptive experience, the one time in their lives when they feel released from the tyranny of the Do It Now. This is the giddiness, the sense of permission that pregnancy bestows, when just to be—to eat, breathe, and sleep—is to do. In the great while of her pregnancy, my mother read *War and Peace* from beginning to end. Then she read it again, from the end to the beginning. Finally—a day or so before my sister's birth—she finished reading it from the middle outward to both ends. There was no gap between the amplitude of the book, her sense of time, her belly.

And isn't the richness of the while one of the primary pleasures of childhood? To lie in the backseat of the car, listening to the grown-ups' voices, while a parent's hands steer through the dark night. To play in the vacant lot at dusk, while through the lighted kitchen window, a mother stands at the stove cooking dinner. The childhood experience of errands, the dreamy, slightly edgy boredom of waiting while the grown-ups drop off mail, pick up the freshly pressed clothes, fill the car with gas—wasn't this, too, a kind of luxury?

When I asked a friend to write about the lost while her thoughts went immediately to childhood: "I grew up reading while my mother cooked, while my brother played, while my father tumbled rocks or made cabernet or carved decoys, depending on which era of hobby he then inhabited. The dog and the cats hung loose and just were. We were an abundance. We were in abundance."

My friend wrote this against the backdrop of a sense of scarcity. Recently divorced, her own sense of scarcity arises from the new experience of living alone. Even though her house is filled with living things—she has a dog, cats, birds, and a burgeoning garden—without the sense of family, she experiences time in her house as a jarring succession of moments:

Living alone one seeks out whiles with a fierceness born of survival instinct. While the radio plays all is not lost. Classical music whiles away time in an orderly way. Sometimes Sophie the dog is too scared that I will be leaving soon to contribute to the while. Lira the cat, and the lovebirds too. The dog whines instantly at the door so that I can't do something while she frolics outdoors, the cat yelps at the bifold door, the birds cry from their cage and I am bombarded by the deepest roots of this floating anxiety: a homelessness within the walls of my supposed home.

Yet, with the dispersal of schedules that characterizes contemporary family life, even people who don't live alone tend not to inhabit each other's whiles. The alarm clocks ring and parents and children scatter, often not to be reunited until the day has grown dark again. And even when they are gathered back under the same roof, it is more and more common for each to be tuned to a different medium: telephone, television, computer screen. If there is a music of family life, it is less and less like a rich and resonating chord than like a pattern of disparate melodic lines occasionally, randomly intersecting. Already Willa Cather's description of a winter evening in Nebraska begins to seem like the record of an alien life form:

> Our lives centered around warmth and food and the return of the men at nightfall. I used to wonder, when they came in tired from the fields, their feet numb and their hands cracked and sore, how they could do all the chores so conscientiously: feed and water and bed the horses, milk the cows, and look after the pigs. When supper was over, it took them a long while to get the cold out of their bones. While grandmother and I washed the dishes and grandfather read his paper upstairs, Jake and Otto sat on the long bench behind the stove, "easing" their inside boots, or rubbing mutton tallow into their cracked hands. . . .

If we no longer inhabit each other's whiles, we also do not inhabit the while of the natural world around us. One evening, as a group of women sat writing around my kitchen table, one woman wrote the words "My own yard stands neglected." Another woman, writing of the tree in her backyard, began with the words, "For too long I have neglected my apples . . . " These two lines, so seemingly mild, held such power for all the women at the table that they began to write spontaneously in response to them. What emerged was writing of extraordinary intensity, expressive of what could only be called a kind of collective grief—a grief at being unable to tend, except in the most rushed, erratic way, to the sphere of life around them. Between the need to earn money and the most necessary errands of practical existence, their waking hours are consumed. The richness of the natural while—leaves falling, weeds sprouting, apples ripening—must be squeezed into a kind of frantic, makeshift parentheses.

"The beauty of hitchhiking," a friend told me recently—he was speaking with nostalgia about the cross-continental adventures of his youth—

> is when you go through the feeling of being at the mercy of circumstance. It's the same feeling as when your car breaks down in the middle of nowhere. You go through that initial panic, that anxiety: *I'm stuck here.* There you are, standing under the big blue sky, no sign of life in any direction. A tumbleweed blows by. You remember that there is still a bit of cheese sandwich at the bottom of your knapsack. You take it out. It's dry and gritty with sand, but it's delicious. You feel free, you feel light as the tumbleweed.

But now, this friend went on to say, we are more and more insulated from such experience. If the car breaks down in the middle of nowhere, we reach for the cellular phone. And notice how this cellular phone—admittedly a true friend in emergency—becomes a small commando in the car, eventually making more and more claims on us. Now there is no excuse not to go on giving and receiving calls, not to fill every interval of life with the business of exchange.

And here is a paradox. The simultaneity of paradise—where desire and fulfillment are one—is a simultaneity in which we can rest, loaf, play. For the world has already been made. It is whole and complete, and on the sixth day of creation, God said, *"Kitov"*: it is good. But the simultaneity of our own ingenuity is one that gives us no rest. The magic machine that can be used anywhere, anytime, becomes the injunction to use it anywhere, anytime; one labor-saving device after another simply opens the horizon of an infinite "to do."

This is not the circle of perfection, but the line, infinitely extending. This is digital time: a succession of undifferentiated moments. When 12:00 flashes, it looks no different than 12:01 or 2:23—and we've entered a different world from that of the circular clock, where at high noon, the hands come together and point upward, toward the sun at its highest point.

This undifferentiated time is the zone of planning. *To plan:* the word is related to the geographical plain, the palm of the hand, to that which is open, flat. This is the terrain that the eye travels over easily. *I can read you like the palm of my hand,* we say, and we would like to read our own lives that way—lines stretching out on a broad surface, marked on the grid of our personal planners.

But what of the time that can't be so clearly accounted for, the time that falls off the thin sheet of the map, the hidden time, not of the plain but rather the cave, or the valley? This is the girl curled in fetal position at the foot of the bed, this is pouch-time, womb-time.

And we have no time for it.

When I was a girl, the season of Lent had a mysterious power all its own. It was the power of interiority. The time when Jesus fell off the map of public life and withdrew into the desert. Forty days of rock and sky. Fasting. One year I gave up sweetened cereals. One year I gave up speaking French, so as to be more ordinary. In church, the statues were wrapped in purple cloth. Resplendent invisibility. Underground, the bulbs were pushing up out of their brown papery skins. Soon it would be spring, flowers blooming, the tabernacle full again after the startling emptiness of Holy Saturday, the statues looking naked in their marble clothes.

Throughout history, differentiation has been at the very core of the human experience of time. The ancient stone monuments of Stonehenge or Carnac catch the shadows that fall on the most extraordinary days of the year: the solstice, the equinox. Pre-industrial village life, tribal life, is under the sway of day and night, heat and cold, drought and rain, seed and fruit. Religious practice, everywhere and from the beginning, involves a pattern of time, an alternation of ordinary and holy days, of sacred and profane.

But increasingly, we live in the twenty-four-hour time of commerce, of convenience, where cash may be obtained, objects ordered from a catalog, stocks exchanged at any time of the day or night. It is 7–11 time, the fluorescent time of unmodulated, shadowless light, where coffee and doughnuts are available at all hours, and the rhythm of breakfast, lunch, and dinner has no meaning. This is money-time, for money, the abstract commodity—unlike baskets of shells or bushels of corn which must be lugged and bartered—has a life of its own. *Ab-stract:* to take out of. This is the glory of money— its detachability from the thick of human life. It is hard for us now to grasp the original shock at the concept of interest, the idea of usury as sin. But the notion that money might accumulate, quite apart from the rhythm of human effort, has had radical consequences for the way we live.

Here is the thrill again, the return to paradise, to a place where money does grow on trees. But here, too, is that strange glissando: that moment where a *can* becomes a *must,* and the realization that money can be made all the time, even when we are sleeping, becomes the injunction to turn all hours into wakeful, productive hours, under the glare of the flourescent lights, in the shadowless realm of the 7–11, where morning is night and Sunday is Monday.

There is another place with the same shrill, twenty-four light, the doors that never shut, the windowless air, and a counter or front desk manned by the same rotation of pale clerks with their free-floating body clocks: the emergency room. What does it mean that the 7–11 and the emergency room are so atmospherically similar?

The emergency room is the true domain of necessity, the place where there is no-drawing-back before the bleeding wound, the broken bone, the last-minute contractions. But a Pop-Tart, a six-pack of Coke in the middle of the night? We have come to believe that convenience is necessity. What begins as slogan, words sprayed on the surface of things—billboards, labels, magazines—becomes visceral, and if we can't find it *now* we feel a knot of anxiety, frustration. We are thrown back on a world that has its own rhythms, that doesn't immediately bend to meet our yen to eat a candy bar or have a shirt pressed—or even our more serious needs. This is one of the most difficult adjustments for Americans traveling abroad: the locked doors at midday, deserted shops on holidays, the need to wait for gas or cash. Our definition of a world in order is one in which all goods and services are always immediately available. This is the paradisical aspect of the mall, and it is our version of eternity: seasonless, ever present, abundant. This is a very different world from one whose order arises from an alternation of presence and absence, scarcity and abundance, winter and spring.

Although we feel anxiety when what we crave is not available, the twenty-four-hour availability of that which we crave does not really provide pleasure. We really are so constituted as to be more responsive to difference than sameness. The hot-cross buns eaten once, at the beginning of Lent, the statues unwrapped from their purple cloth in the hours before Easter, the seasonal truffles—black gold of France—eaten in the first chill of October. It remains true for us that hunger is the best spice, and intense sensual pleasure, like gratitude, is the opposite of taking for granted.

The French, with their great love for food, have long hours when the kitchen is off bounds, the larder closed. The notion of all-day all-you-can-eat, of simply wandering into the kitchen, opening the door of the refrigerator and staring blankly into its contents, wondering, "What do I feel like eating now?" would strike them as quite foreign. If you ride on a French train, you will notice at a certain hour in late afternoon that the passengers begin one by one, in their separate seats, to unwrap their chocolate bars, their packages of biscuits. . . . No bell has sounded, but through the whir of the train's wheels and in the taste of the chocolate and biscuit, there is an acute pleasure. Munching one's *gouter,* one is doing one's part to keep the world simultaneously moving forward and on track.

There is a pleasure in rebelling, too—eating dessert first, having breakfast in the middle of the night—but only over or against a sense of order. Otherwise, there is just a kind of vacuum, the emptiness of availability, the sadness of drinks at the bar at 10 A.M. As Camus said, "The hardest thing is to give up what we don't really want."

It is no small thing to be liberated from the alternations of necessity, the relentless demands of the seasons, the times of scarcity and cold. We work hard, in the sweat of our brow, to gain a sense of predictability and control, the sense of having the goods of the world on tap, at any time of the night or day.

But, in the words of my hitchhiking friend, "Each time we make another incursion of will into the world, we lose another opportunity to feel what's on the other side of helplessness—our place in the world." And what he meant by that was a sense of being buoyed, sustained by something bigger than what we ourselves can achieve.

One night not long ago, I brought this poem of James Wright to a group of women I know:

LYING IN A HAMMOCK AT WILLIAM DUFFY'S FARM IN PINE ISLAND, MINNESOTA

Over my head, I see the bronze butterfly,
Asleep on the black trunk,
Blowing like a leaf in green shadow.
Down the ravine behind the empty house,
The cowbells follow one another
Into the distances of the afternoon.
To my right,
In a field of sunlight between two pines,
The droppings of last year's horses
Blaze up into golden stones.
I lean back, as the evening darkens and comes on.
A chicken hawk floats over, looking for home.
I have wasted my life.

"That's tragic!" one of the women said when I had finished reading. In her eyes, this was a man who was better off dead. For her, the conventional meaning of the last line obliterated all that preceded it, the images of a world taking care of itself, simultaneously self-contained and overflowing, a world where nothing is lost, where distance is always gathered back into nearness, and where dung blazes up like gold. In such a world, it is possible to swing in a hammock, suspended in air, and realize that a lifetime of anxious effort has been utterly foolish—a waste. What a marvelous joke! All the more so, because in the moment of realization, the wasted life—along with the sleeping butterfly, the sound of the cowbells, and the chicken hawk—is one more treasure.

For a moment I didn't know what to say to my friend. She was so adamant. I found myself looking at the scar on her face. It's a small scar, but it is the result of rather complicated neurological surgery that she required after one of the many times that her husband struck her. She had just left this man, with whom she had lived for fifteen years. She had a young daughter to support, and the two of them had just moved into the house where we had gathered. Earlier in the evening, she had spoken with horror about her desire to sleep. "All I want to do is sleep all day," she said, making an expression of acute disgust.

And then I looked up. I saw that, above us on the mantle, was a large framed print of Andrew Wyeth's called "Sleep." It shows a woman, a box of berries beside her, lying in a meadow of gold grass. She has flung herself down with complete abandon, and the hard ground has received her, become soft for her, as if she always slept in a bed of grass, like a deer. Seeing that my friend had given this painting—and not the Do It Now—the place of honor in her new house, I wondered why we banish ourselves from such moments again and again.

ISHMAEL REED

Progress: A Faustian Bargain

In order to justify its programs, NASA, in its brochures, describes the earth as a dying planet, a fact which for them justifies colonizing the universe. Given the mess that's been made of this planet in the name of progress, you can understand why, in many science fiction movies, the goal of the invaders is to destroy the planet, lest this progress be extended to their neighborhoods. Many say that we are reaching the point of no return, beyond which the salvaging of the planet will be impossible, and in September 1997 a number of Nobel laureates signed an urgent warning about human-influenced climate change. Their claims are dismissed as hysterical by spokespersons employed by the fossil fuels industry, which has undertaken the kind of public relations campaign that led to the defeat of Hillary Clinton's health proposals. Another environmentalist warned that at our rate of growth less food will be grown in the next forty years than in the last eight thousand. These prophecies and others lend credence to Richard Leakey's warning that man is on the brink of extinction. He said that "Global warming, loss of the rain forests, industrial pollution of the waterways, depletion of the ozone layer, and the spread of AIDS were among the factors that were potential threats to the species."

How did we reach this disaster? I would suggest that it can be traced to a perverted notion of progress, a word that, according to the American Heritage Dictionary, is chiefly British. England was the scene of the Industrial Revolution, which led to the chemical revolution and other dangerous "progressive" solutions, mostly heralded for their benefits to mankind or as "time-saving devices," and for their ability to make our lives more convenient. The countries where these revolutions have taken place hold them up to the rest of the nations as proof of their superiority. If you don't have this gadgetry, they say, then you are "underdeveloped" or even "backward." On the day that Rover landed on Mars and began transmitting pictures, white sportscasters were gloating over the fact that Mike Tyson had chomped off part of Evander Holyfield's ear. The juxtaposition of those images said it all. While white men are reaching the stars, the rest of us are cannibals. We're still saying "B'Wana" in the Tarzan movies. Even though black scientists are responsible for inventing some of the most avant garde of space equipment, Norman Mailer, in his book *Fire on the Moon,* said that such space shots emasculated us primitives. After the O. J. Simpson trial, Mailer said that African Americans supported the defendant because we are less rational than whites. If a "progressive" thinks this way, you can imagine how the others think.

But as our fish develop sores and die as a result of pollution, as our air becomes dirtier, as the ozone is depleted over Antarctica, our devotion to progress can be viewed as a Faustian bargain. All one has to do is visit the Peace Museum at Hiroshima to understand that one person's progress is another person's hell.

The twentieth century has witnessed a marriage of heaven and hell. Millions of people live in a style that was available only to the elites of former times, indeed, to kings and queens. Mass production of inexpensive books has made literacy more available to the average person than it was to Shakespeare, who lived in a time when the best books were locked away by the elite. You can walk up Telegraph Avenue in Berkeley, or Broadway near Lincoln Center in New York, and sidewalk hawkers will sell you literary classics for a dime, and used CDs of Beethoven's last quartets, and John Coltrane playing soprano saxophone, for a little more. State subsidies make dance and theatre available to millions and, with Internet search engines, more information can be had in your home than was available to colleges and universities in the last thousand years.

Great strides have been made in medicine, sparing millions the scourge of diseases which in a former time devastated whole populations. Incredible moral and political revolutions were wrought by Gandhi and Martin Luther King, Jr., without their firing a single shot.

But while men and women have behaved brilliantly in this century, they have also been stupid, venal, vile, and even wicked. Even though the so called Cold War has ended, the manufacturing of newer, more sophisticated nuclear weapons continues. Scenes of horror and mass destruction and extermination are broadcast on television, interrupted only by the hawking of products. Mass murders in Indonesia, Rwanda, and Cambodia vie with those of the World Wars in their enormity. Jason Epstein says that these grim atrocities may only be a preparation for even more horrible holocausts that will take place in the twenty-first century. So inevitable is human progress that perhaps by the middle of the twenty-first century each person will own a custom-made mass grave. The fashion industry will vanish, because the only attire required in the next century will be a biohazard suit and an oxygen tank.

In the United States, plagues, both natural and man-made, devastate whole neighborhoods. Even though the media flatter the entity they refer to as "white America" by blaming these catastrophes on the lack of moral character among the black and brown populations, social pathologies are rife in the suburbs as well. While "out-of-wedlock" births among blacks have declined drastically, those among the white population are soaring (yet black pathology merchants from think tanks and journalism still write about rising out-of-wedlock births when even Ben Wattenberg of the American Enterprise Institute says it's not so). The *Philadelphia Inquirer* reported that heroin abuse in the suburbs is skyrocketing. Yet the media continue to blame the drug trade on black foot soldiers, which is like blaming drugstore clerks for the Phen-Fen diet pill scandal. A whole industry has emerged, based on the scolding of blacks and devoted to the idea that racism no longer exists. One of those who've hit the jackpot is *New Yorker* writer Joe Klein. He says that so impoverished are the moral values of the inner cities that they should be turned over to the churches. When is the last time that Joe Klein read the Bible, where, if you really want to read some invective, check out Jesus Christ holding forth on hypocrisy. Joe Klein was one of the biggest liars of the 1990s. He's not the only one. One of the governors who has been praised for cutting "immoral" welfare recipients off food stamps and other subsidies made the short list for vice presidential nominees during the last campaign. His name was dropped from the list when it was revealed that he was supporting his mistress from his wife's bank account. An elitist magazine editor who recommended to blacks that they adhere to bourgeois values was found to be a dedicated cocaine addict, and the founder of supply-side economics who used to appear on *Wall Street Week* and scorn money spent on social programs was so spaced out on the drug that his wife had to petition for the right to control his estate. I could go on.

This century has proven that technology, arrogance, and ignorance are a lethal concoction. Now they tell us that the nuclear fallout from their crazy tests has infected thousands with cancer. Forty years after the fact they tell us that poor blacks and whites were used in plutonium experiments. Maybe forty years from now they will admit that they cooperated with organized crime and international hoodlums who brought drugs into our country, murdering the souls of millions and destroying not only the neighborhoods that were targeted, but also the suburbs. They tell us that people who look like them are the brightest and the best: Aristotle, whose views on women are stupid, or Diderot, a racist, and Voltaire, an anti-Semite and a racist. As soon as Microsoft, the state-of-the-art company in cyberspace, went on-line they had to apologize for referring to Indians as savages, a good example of the canyon that exists between our knowledge of objects and our knowledge of one another. Maybe our truncated knowledge of the world is the result of the "great books" canon, which includes not one Asian, African, or a European woman.

Once in a while we get a glimpse of the philosophy guiding the corporate-owned politicians who sell us their masters' final product, gleaming in the political showrooms. What's behind the Contract with America, Proposition 187, Proposition 209, the growing prison industry, the welfare bill, mandatory sentencing, the prohibition against clean needles, and reduction and elimination of services for the elderly and the disabled?

The American Psychological Association was about to honor Raymond B. Cattell until the Anti-Defamation League reminded them of some of his racist writings. Mr. Cattell believes that "poverty and disease are part of the natural selection process that keeps a race healthy. Modern social welfare simply abolishes the checks natural selection imposes on biological systems." Cattell and his friends regard Christianity as "a denial of the urge to evolution, 'encouraging' the increase of the unfit." How do we deal with the unfit? By using "genthanasia," a "phasing out" in which a moribund culture is ended. Immigration, for Cattell, only draws "people of low genetic quality." The American Psychological Association saluted Mr. Cattell for his "lifetime contribution in the public interest." Well, Mr. Cattell, who said in 1994 that Hitler actually shared many values of the average American, may have tapped into the zeitgeist. Charles Murray's book *The Bell Curve,* which includes similar arguments, and was partially financed by the Pioneer Fund, whose Nazi ties have been documented, was favorably received even by the *New York Times Book Review.*

It's hard to disagree with animal photographer Peter Beard, who, while lamenting the vanishing elephant herds, said that humans are the most greedy and selfish animals in the animal kingdom, an animal that began the twentieth century with an ugly circus of carnage called World War I, and toward the end of the century was speculating about how to phase out unwanted groups through genthanasia. To some, that's progress.

KIRKPATRICK SALE

Five Facets of a Myth

I can vividly remember sitting at the dinner table arguing with my father about progress, using on him all the experience and wisdom I had gathered at the age of fifteen. Of course we live in an era of progress, I said, just look at cars—how clumsy and unreliable and slow they were in the old days, how sleek and efficient and speedy they are now.

He raised an eyebrow, just a little. And what has been the result of having all these wonderful new sleek and efficient and speedy cars? he asked. I was taken aback. I searched for a way to answer. He went on.

How many people die each year as a result of these speedy cars? How many are maimed and crippled? What is life like for the people who produce them, on those famous assembly lines, the same routinized job hour after hour, day after day, like in Chaplin's film? How many fields and forests and even towns and villages have been paved over so that these cars can get to all the places they want to get to—and park there? Where does all the gasoline come from, and at what cost, and what happens when we burn it and exhaust it?

Thankfully, before I could stammer out a response, he went on to tell me about an article written on the subject of progress, a concept I had never really thought of, by one of his Cornell colleagues, the historian Carl Becker, a man I had never heard of, in the *Encylopedia of Social Sciences,* a resource I had never come across. Read it, he said.

I'm afraid it was another fifteen years before I did, though in the meantime I came to learn the wisdom of my father's skepticism as the modern world repeatedly threw up other examples of invention and advancement—television, electric carving knife, microwave oven, nuclear power—that showed the same problematic nature of progress, taken in the round and negatives factored in, as did the automobile. When I finally got to Becker's masterful essay, in the course of a wholesale re-examination of modernity, it took no scholarly armament of his to convince me of the peculiar historical provenance of the concept of progress and its status not as an inevitability, a force as given as gravity as my youthful self imagined, but as a cultural construct invented for all practical purposes in the Renaissance, and which advanced the propaganda of capitalism. It was nothing more than a serviceable myth, a deeply held, unexamined construct—like all useful cultural myths—that promoted the idea of regular and eternal improvement of the human condition, largely through the exploitation of nature and the acquisition of material goods.

Of course by now it is no longer such an arcane perception. Many fifteen year olds today, seeing clearly the perils that have accompanied modern technology in its progress, some of which perils threaten the very continuance of the human species, have already worked out for themselves what's wrong with the myth. It is hard to learn that forests are being cut down at the rate of 56 million acres a year, that desertification threatens 8 billion acres of land worldwide, that all of the world's 17 major fisheries are in decline and stand a decade away from virtual exhaustion, that 26 million tons of topsoil is lost to erosion and pollution every year, and believe that the world's economic system, whose functioning exacts this price, is headed in the right direction and that that direction should be labeled "progress."

E. E. Cummings once called progress a "comfortable disease" of modern "manunkind," and so it has been for some. But at any time since the triumph of capitalism only a minority of the world's population could be said to be really living in comfort, and that comfort, continuously threatened, is achieved at considerable expense.

Today, of the approximately 6 billion people in the world, it is estimated that at least a billion live in abject poverty, their lives cruel, empty, and mercifully short. Another 2 billion eke out life on a bare subsistence level, usually sustained only by one or another starch, the majority without potable water or sanitary toilets. More than 2 billion more live at the bottom edges of the money economy, with incomes less than $5,000 a year and no property or savings, no net worth to pass on to their children. That leaves less than a billion people who even come close to struggling for lives of comfort, with jobs and salaries of some regularity, and a quite small minority at the top of that scale who could really be said to have achieved comfortable lives. In the world, some 350 people can be considered (U.S. dollar) billionaires (with slightly more than 3 million millionaires), and their total net worth is estimated to exceed that of 45 percent of the world's population.

This is progress? A disease such a small number can catch? And with such inequity, such imbalance?

In the United States, the most materially advanced nation in the world and long the most ardent champion of the notion of progress, some 40 million people live below the official poverty line and another 20 million or so below the line adjusted for real costs; 6 million or so are unemployed, more than 30 million are said to be too discouraged to look for work, and 45 million are in "disposable" jobs, temporary and part-time, without benefits or security. The top 5 percent of the population owns about two-thirds of the total wealth; 60 percent own no tangible assets or are in debt; in terms of income, the top 20 percent earn half the total income, the bottom 20 percent less than 4 percent of it.

All this hardly suggests the sort of material comfort progress is assumed to have provided. Certainly many in the United States and throughout the industrial world live at levels of wealth undreamed of in ages past, able to call forth hundreds of servant-equivalents at the flip of a switch or turn of a key, and probably a third of this "First

World" population could be said to have lives of ease and convenience. Yet it is a statistical fact that it is just this segment that most acutely suffers from the *true* "comfortable disease," what I would call *affluenza:* heart disease, stress, overwork, family dysfunction, alcoholism, insecurity, anomie, psychosis, loneliness, impotence, alienation, consumerism, and coldness of heart.

Leopold Kohr, the Austrian economist whose seminal work *The Breakdown of Nations* is an essential tool for understanding the failures of political progress in the last half-millennium, often used to close his lectures with this analogy.

Suppose we are on a progress-train, he said, running full speed ahead in the approved manner, fueled by rapacious growth and resource depletion and cheered on by highly rewarded economists. What if we then discover that we are headed for a precipitous fall to certain disaster just a few miles ahead when the tracks end at an uncrossable gulf? Do we take the advice of the economists to put more fuel into the engines so that we go at an ever faster rate, presumably hoping that we build up a head of steam so powerful that it can land us safely on the other side of the gulf; or do we reach for the brakes and come to a screeching if somewhat tumble-around halt as quickly as possible?

Progress is the myth that assures us that full speed ahead is never wrong. Ecology is the discipline that teaches us that it is disaster.

Before the altar of progress, attended by its dutiful acolytes of science and technology, modern industrial society has presented an increasing abundance of sacrifices from the natural world, imitating on a much grander and more devastating scale the religious rites of earlier empires built on similar conceits about the domination of nature. Now, it seems, we are prepared to offer up even the very biosphere itself.

No one knows how resilient the biosphere is, how much damage it is able to absorb before it stops functioning—or at least functioning well enough to keep the human species alive. But in recent years some very respectable and authoritative voices have suggested that, if we continue the relentless rush of progress that is so stressing the earth on which it depends, we will reach that point in the quite near future. The Worldwatch Institute, which issues annual accountings of such things, has warned that there is not one life-support system on which the biosphere depends for its existence—healthy air, water, soil, temperature, and the like—that is not now severely threatened and in fact getting worse decade by decade. Not long ago a gathering of elite environmental scientists and activists in Morelia, Mexico, published a declaration warning of "environmental destruction" and expressing unanimous concern "that life on our planet is in grave danger." And recently the U.S. Union of Concerned Scientists, in a statement endorsed by more than a hundred Noble laureates and 1,600 members of national academies of science all over the world, proclaimed a "World Scientists' Warning to Humanity" stating that the present rates of environmental assault and population increase cannot continue without "vast human misery" and a planet so "irretrievably mutilated" that "it will be unable to sustain life in the manner that we know."

The high-tech global economy will not listen; cannot listen. It continues apace its expansion and exploitation. Thanks to it, human beings annually use up some 40 percent of all the net photosynthetic energy available to the planet Earth, though we are but a single species of comparatively insignificant numbers. The world economy has grown by more than five times in the last fifty years and is continuing at a dizzying pace to use up the world's resources, create unabating pollution and waste, and increase the enormous inequalities within and between all nations of the world.

Suppose an objective observer were to measure the success of Progress—that is, the capital-P myth that ever since the Enlightenment has nurtured and guided and presided over that happy marriage of science and capitalism that has produced modern industrial civilization.

Has it been, on the whole, better or worse for the human species? Other species? Has it brought humans more happiness than there was before? More justice? More equality? More efficiency? And if its ends have proven to be more benign than not, what of its means? At what price have its benefits been won? And are they sustainable?

The objective observer would have to conclude that the record is mixed, at best. On the plus side, there is no denying that material prosperity has increased for about a sixth of the world's humans, for some beyond the most avaricious dreams of kings and potentates of the past. The world has developed systems of transportation and communication that allow people, goods, and information to be exchanged on a scale and at a swiftness never before possible. And for maybe a third of these humans longevity has been increased, along with a general improvement in health and sanitation that has allowed the expansion of human numbers about tenfold in the last three centuries.

On the minus side, the costs have been considerable. The impact on the earth's species and systems of providing prosperity for a billion people has been, as we have seen, devastatingly destructive—only one additional measure of which is the fact that it has meant the permanent extinction of perhaps 500,000 species in this century alone. The impact on the remaining five-sixths of the human species has been likewise destructive, as most of them have seen their societies colonized or displaced, their economies wrenched and shattered, and their environments transformed for the worse, driving them into deprivation and misery that are almost certainly worse than those they ever knew, however difficult their times past, before the advent of industrial society.

And even the billion whose living standards use up what is effectively 100 percent of the world's available resources each year, and who might be therefore assumed to be happy as a result, do not in fact seem to be so. No social indices in any advanced society suggest that people are more content than they were a generation ago. Various surveys indicate that the "misery quotient" in most countries has increased, and considerable real-world evidence (such as rising rates of mental illness, drugs, crime, divorce, and depression) argues that the results of material enrichment have not included much individual happiness.

Indeed, on a larger scale, almost all that Progress was supposed to achieve has failed to come about, despite the immense amount of money and technology devoted to its cause. Virtually all of the dreams that have adorned it over the years, particularly in its most robust stages in the late nineteenth century and in the past twenty years of computerdom, have dissipated as utopian fancies—those that have not, like nuclear power, chemical agriculture, manifest destiny, and the welfare state, turned into nightmares. Progress has not, even in this most progressive nation, eliminated poverty (the number of poor has increased and real income has declined for twenty-five years). It has not eliminated drudgery (hours of employment have increased, as has work within the home, for both sexes). It has not eliminated ignorance (literacy rates have declined for fifty years, and test scores have declined). It has not eliminated disease (hospitalization, illness, and death rates have all increased since 1980).

It seems quite simple; beyond prosperity and longevity, and those limited to a minority, and each with seriously damaging environmental consequences, Progress does not have a great deal going for it. For its adherents, of course, it is probably sufficient that wealth is meritorious and affluence desirable and longer life positive. The terms of the game for them are simple: material betterment for as many as possible, as fast as possible. Nothing else, certainly not considerations of personal morality or social cohesion or spiritual depth or participatory government, seems much to matter.

But the objective observer is not so narrow-minded, and is able to see how deep and deadly are the shortcomings of such a view. The objective observer could only conclude that since the fruits of Progress are so meager, the price by which they have been won is far too high, in social, economic, political, and environmental terms, and that neither the societies nor ecosystems of the world will be able to bear the cost for more than a few decades longer, if they have not already been damaged beyond redemption.

Herbert Read, the British philosopher and critic, once wrote that "only a people serving an apprenticeship to nature can be trusted with machines." It is a profound insight, and he underscored it by adding that "only such people will so contrive and control those machines that their products are an enhancement of biological needs, and not a denial of them."

An apprenticeship to nature—now *there's* a myth a stable and durable society could live by.

PORTER SHREVE

Made by You

At the corner of Germantown and Springfield Avenues in the Mount Airy neighborhood of Philadelphia there used to be a four-story, turn-of-the-century federal with a flagstone courtyard and a garden. Though I've never been back, I imagine it's still there.

The best days of my parents' marriage began in the late spring of 1973, when my father received a start-up grant to open an alternative school and took possession of this house. My mother would soon be pregnant with their fourth child. We lived in a cosy fieldstone cottage a few blocks away, with both of my grandmothers, my uncle Jeff, and the remaining three hippies from a small commune Jeff had formed in Colorado.

My father, well liked around the city because he had been the star of the University of Pennsylvania football team during its few winning years, was someone to whom people had always felt generosity. When he was growing up, teachers, coaches, and neighbors had pitched in, sending him to private school and summer camp and college. Something about him—his modesty, his father's early death, the fact that he was a spectacular athlete who sang in the choir and embarrassed easily—brought forth good will. It was appropriate, then, that a near-stranger named Woodward, who owned hundreds of houses in North Philadelphia, including the one we lived in, would on the day my father received his grant hand him a ring of keys, saying, "As long as you're starting a school, you're going to need a schoolhouse."

Rent free, with a one-year renewable lease. A tall beige-colored stucco on a charming street in one of the most ethnically diverse neighborhoods in the country. With help from Crosby, Stills, and Nash, my father named the school, "Our House," as in "Our house is a very very very fine house / With two cats in the yard, life used to be so hard. . . ." He advertised in the Mount Airy and Chesnut Hill community papers and posted flyers around local schools, and by the end of summer a hundred students had enrolled.

Nineteen seventy-three was the year of the Vietnam cease-fire agreement. I was seven years old, and like everyone else in the house I wore an aluminum bracelet with a soldier's name stenciled across it and watched the papers for the soldier's return. The year before, Nixon had won reelection in a near record landslide, and many young people felt that the sixties had passed them by and that the seventies threatened a return to the unenlightened past. Philadelphia crawled with runaways and dropouts and students for whom traditional education no longer held an interest.

"Our House" welcomed them all.

For some, it provided an after-school program. The schools they went to didn't offer classes in such fine arts as photography, painting and drawing, music, and creative writing. Or their high school courses and textbooks had yet to adjust to the changes of the past ten years. At "Our House" they could take any number of arts courses, plus feminist literature, religions of the world, Indian myths, and urban cultures.

For others, the school fostered community. Many evenings, guests would come—musicians, poets and writers, craftspeople, sociologists, ministers from urban churches—and stand in front of the fireplace playing instruments or lecturing, taking questions from the students, who sat cross-legged on the floor or slouched on comfortable couches. The first floor had another large room, used as a gallery space for students and local artisans to display and sell their work. The walls and tables were filled with pottery, wooden toys, candles, crystals, and dream catchers, macramé, batiking, weaving, and tie-dye, paintings, photographs, stained glass, and poetry chapbooks. Revenue from the gallery and the gallery coffee bar, which did a brisk business, went a long way toward making "Our House" self-sufficient. Everyone had a special craft, each contributing a small part to the whole.

Besides serving as the school's administrator, my father taught the course in urban cultures. He'd take his class of fifteen students to South Philadelphia, where they'd meet and talk with people in the neighborhoods—aldermen, civic leaders, Baptist ministers, Polish deli owners, Italian barbers. They'd study the architecture of both Independence Hall and the Gloria Dei church. They'd see Rothkos at the Museum of American Art and study graffiti under the bridges on Snyder Avenue, asking kids at inner-city playgrounds to explain the symbolism.

My mother, fresh off the publication of her first novel, taught creative writing and modern American poetry, and my Uncle Jeff, who had been a National Outdoor Leadership instructor out West, ran a course in wilderness education, taking his students around the Wissahickon, down the Shenandoah, through the city parks. My younger brother and sister and I never needed child care. We had two live-in grandmothers and a school of our own.

The sister with whom my mother was pregnant that year turns twenty-four tomorrow. I've flown from Michigan to Washington, D.C., where the family moved after Philadelphia and a brief stop in Texas, to celebrate her birthday. She lives in Providence, my middle brother in Denver, my middle sister in New York City. I'm in Ann Arbor. This will be the first time we'll all be together in six months.

I'm fairly good about keeping up with my sisters. One I talk with every week and the other every two weeks. We often "speak" by e-mail, paragraph answered by one-liner, one-liner answered by paragraph, using a clipped jargon that feels almost natural but is utterly unlike the way we think or speak or write, as if there's a glib censor we all have to pass through. E-mail makes us feel satisfied that we're adequately in touch even when many of our messages are those weedlike forwarded jokes or good-luck totems or political pleas that none of us probably has the time to read anyway. I can't remember the last time I got an actual letter. I still trot out of my bachelor apartment into the Michigan cold half-expecting some real correspondence among my bills and magazines and sweepstakes, but the likelihood of a handwritten letter these days—and I realize it's half my fault—is on the level of actually winning the promised ten million dollars.

My brother, like my father in the years that followed the divorce, may as well be living on the moons of Jupiter.

It would be nice if he gave me his new e-mail address or if he still worked for that company with the sky pagers. I used to call an 800 number and leave little messages that would buzz his hip and tick across a tiny screen: "Nice haircut"; "Call if you get married"; "Reminder: bigamy is illegal in your state." But I rarely heard back and my jokes got worse and I'd see him four times a year and we'd spend most of the time promising better communication.

In the communication age, the most difficult people to communicate with are those you care most about.

I'm here a day before the others and need to find a birthday gift.

"You have to see this exhibit down at the Sackler," my mother tells me, referring to the Smithsonian Gallery of Asian Art.

"I think I'll wait for the others and we'll all go tomorrow," I say.

"You could literally spend days there," she says. "The detail is that astonishing. It's called 'The King of the World.'"

Always, after the initial euphoria of coming home and seeing my mother and stepfather and the three dogs, one of them orphaned by me and the other by my birthday sister, my heart sinks a little. I notice the fresh-cut flowers in every room and the stocked refrigerator and the new books carefully chosen and placed on all the tables and the stereo playing something cheerful and festive. Even the dogs have had a bath. My aged basset hound's teeth sparkle.

Most people my age say their parents were glad when they left the house. "They couldn't wait to get rid of me," they say.

"I don't believe it," I tell them. "Our parents came of age in the sixties. It was all about extending the family back then."

"Not anymore." They laugh. "Last time I went home they had converted my room into a sauna."

My mother would never change any of our rooms. Sometimes she has boarders who keep the beds warm, and always old friends and students passing through. She still carries the spirit of the alternative school. Unlike my father, whose passion for the cooperative ended with "Our House," my mother has always wanted nothing more than to live as we did in 1973. All under a great roof or out in the country somewhere like a Chekhov family in the sunny years before the opening act.

I tell her I'm headed out to buy a gift. She asks if I want company, but I'm feeling melancholy, so I set out alone, down our street towards the subway.

As I'm about to step on the red line escalator I notice a sign across the street where an old barbershop used to be. Every time I come home, our neighborhood strip loses another old standard—The Roma (Since 1927) replaced by a mini-mall; Poor Robert's Tavern gutted and track lit by Egghead software; Bob's Ice Cream Parlor given way to the green ubiquity of Starbucks.

"MADE BY YOU," the sign reads, and in small handwritten letters beneath it, "the paint-your-own-pottery store."

The salesgirl is dour. She wears a lime green and royal blue wide-collar sundress and white patent leather half-boots. One of her eyebrows is pierced. She strikes me as a confluence of late seventies disco and early eighties punk.

"This is neat," I say.

She eyes me in a way that says, "This is retail and I won't indulge you."

"So what do I do? I pick a bowl and start painting? That's all there is to it?"

She nods and leans on the counter, picking up a magazine. Her languid body takes the shape of the letter S.

Not looking up, she says, "There's a free station in the back. Just tell me the colors you want."

I look around for a while, feeling a little square and self-conscious, and soon settle on a white ceramic milk pitcher.

It's just before noon on a Friday, so there aren't many people in the store.

I ask for sky blue, orange, purple, black, green, and beige and settle with my paints at the back station.

I begin with the house—two vertical lines, a pitched roof, large windows on four floors. I paint it beige, with white trim and black shutters. On one side I put a garden with purple flowers, on the other a small lawn. I paint two cats sitting side by side in the high grass—one orange tabby, the other midnight black. Over this scene I fill in blue sky and draw a smiling orange sun near the pitcher spout. On the other side I paint the VW bus my uncle drove from Colorado, which broke down in our driveway as soon as he arrived. I fill the side of the bus with flowers and fauna and mountains and peace signs using every color the bad-tempered girl had given me. In the windows I draw myself and my three siblings, smiling and waving, all of us with long stringy hair. Over the bus, in bubbly green letters, surrounded by purple stars, I write: "OUR HOUSE."

"How long does it take to fire up?" I ask the salesgirl.

"There's a wait." She stifles a yawn.

I look around the near-empty store, but never one to make a fuss, I say nothing.

"Come back this afternoon," she says, punching numbers into the computer. "That's six dollars an hour, plus fifty-five for the pitcher. Your total's sixty-one plus tax." Absently I hand her my credit card, thinking maybe I'll kill the time at the exhibit my mother recommended. I could always go back tomorrow when everyone else arrives.

On the Metro to the Smithsonian I'm pleased with myself. I can't remember the last time I made someone a gift. Probably the coiling ash tray I gave to my grandmother back in sixth grade. There just isn't time anymore. My sister's bureau tilts with the birthday sweaters I've given her. Now I'm giddy for her to open the gift.

Finally something to counter the electronic age, I think. I've been waiting for a backlash against the depersonalizing effects of computers: people escaping into themselves, creating fictive personas on the Internet, avoiding human contact through voice mail and e-mail, having secret relationships with multiple faceless strangers, as real and tactile as letters across a keyboard. Virtual reality, the virtual classroom, every lifestyle and interest subdivided into its own private chaos.

Co-opted metaphors like chat "rooms" and "windows" and industry-planted catch phrases like "global community" turn me positively old-fashioned. The computer is no house, its community an abstraction. The information age is a retreat from the heart to the mind. And the mind can be cold and dangerous.

So when I think of "Made by You" I am hopeful. "Make your own pottery" seems to recognize a need for human, face-to-face connection again. A return to the personal, me to you.

At the entrance to the "King of the World" a docent hands me a magnifying glass.

The exhibit is forty-eight pages from the *Padshahnama*, the official history of Shah Jahan, the seventeenth-century Grand Mogul who built the Taj Mahal as a tomb for his favorite wife. All the pictures on the walls were once bound in a single volume—239 folios of text and illustrations.

Many of the illustrations take place at court—Europeans bring gifts to Shah Jahan, Shah Jahan honoring Prince Dara-Shikoh at his wedding, the weighing of Shah Jahan on his forty-second lunar birthday. Most striking about these pictures, besides the sumptuous colors and meticulous brushstrokes, is the number of figures in each scene. In "The Weighing," nearly a hundred sheikhs, courtiers, emirs, and holy men preside at the ceremony, all crowded onto two eleven-by-seventeen pages.

I hardly know where to focus my attention. The King of the World stands at the center of the picture in an elegant purple robe, but he is no larger than the rest of the figures nor more lavishly dressed. Taken by the vibrancy of the scene as a whole, the eye can't help wandering.

Soon I'm looking through the magnifying glass—at the individual faces, all of them remarkably different in complexion, pallor, expression, adornment. Some have soft beards, others coarse, some wear earrings. They carry swords or ivory-handled daggers; a few, I see, have slingshots. Their faces are sallow, white, ruddy, many shades of brown. They look, from left to right: sly, bored, distracted, impressed, choleric, devoted, dreamy. Most stand in profile; a few look askance. No two head-wraps are the same. Every color brightens the page—orange, purple, gold, emerald, turquoise, burgundy, silver, white, black, yellow, and the deepest red.

Through the magnifying glass, I look up close at a bejeweled elephant the size of a small teacup. I can see every line in the skin of his trunk, each ring around the bells in his headdress, the pupils in his burnished amber eyes. I find a tapestry hanging behind Shah Jahan and study its rich woven texture, then the gleam in the pearls around a servant's neck, the gold tassels of his sash, his wide hopeful eyes, until I realize I've been standing at this one illustration for twenty minutes and people are lined up behind me.

Late in the afternoon, I'm back on the subway packed in with rush hour. I draw my focus in from the crowd of tired faces—bureaucrats and lawyers, secretaries and clerks in their uniform navies and grays, their wingtips and jogging shoes gripping the floor of the train—*Washington,* I think, *late twentieth-century America,* and suddenly I feel foolish about the gift I've made for my sister.

Shah Jahan, one of history's great patrons of books, knew the artists he had commissioned would take years to finish their lavish illustrations, recognizing that true excellence was worth the wait. I remember seeing in the background of one battle scene a lion, to the naked eye no bigger than a fingernail. Through the magnifying glass I noticed a long gash on the lion's shoulder. He was turning his head around to inspect it. I moved right up close and actually saw flies buzzing around the wound. How could the artist hold his hand that still? And what value have we lost that encouraged such careful attention to detail? Whoever would take the time today? And, just as disturbingly, who would bother to notice?

"Our House," the history of my life as I'd like it to be, the happiest time of my childhood, had taken me less than an hour to paint.

Sixty-one dollars plus tax. I've joined the crowd of the new dilettante—the Made by You generation, where everyone has a personal

Web page, cuts his own CD off downloaded sounds from the Internet, publishes and distributes his random thoughts and poetry in a self-edited zine, shoots his own independent film on a handheld camera, weighs in to an audience of few more than one.

Everyone's talking and nobody cares to listen. Mine's the generation gunning for the individual, where everyone is King of the World. A hundred and fifty channels, each a little different, like the clothes at Urban Outfitters and the placement of your body piercings, yet conforming just the same.

I get off the subway and cross the street and catch the dour salesgirl as she's closing the store.

"You," she says, flatly, walking back inside and returning with a paper bag.

"I guess you don't gift wrap," I say.

She locks the door and walks away.

I head back up the street toward my family's house and remove the pitcher from the bag.

I'm surprised at how much I like it, actually—the cats and the smiling sun, the slightly leaning house. Fired in the oven it looks wonderfully glossy and colorful. I guess I'll give it to her, after all, I think. What a dull curmudgeon I can be. Thirty-one and such a dark view of progress.

I turn the pitcher around and see the bus and the purple words on the back, and then suddenly I realize that the sister whose birthday is tomorrow never even saw "Our House." My mother was still pregnant when we had to give it away. I had always assumed, since the alternative school lived so brightly in my memory, that my youngest sister had been there. We had often talked about it, and she had acted a part.

Just before she was born, my father got a job offer in Houston, so a year after opening the school he handed the keys back to Mr. Woodward and the family packed up, never to return to Philadelphia. My father became a psychologist, my mother and uncle both teachers. One of my grandmothers died that year; the other had emphysema so couldn't follow us to Texas. We became, in 1974, an ordinary American family, our community reduced to us alone.

I look again at the bus and see myself and my three siblings smiling in the window, my youngest sister every bit a part of my happiest memory. In my mother's house there's a fire in the fireplace. The dogs trundle up and sniff my hands. I walk upstairs and set the pitcher on my sister's table and sit in her rocking chair, tick-tocking back and forth, thinking of how I might word the card.

JANNA MALAMUD SMITH

Beyond Bread and Roses

It is rare that I cry at dinner. Certainly not with guests present. I cannot remember what we were eating, or whether the wine was red or white. I don't think I'd had more than a glass all evening, so it is unlikely that these were wine tears. They were, however, startling, unexpected to me as much as to my dinner companions. I had casually set out to talk about James Carroll's sixties-era memoir, *An American Requiem,* which I had just finished reading. Before I knew it, I was crying about the Vietnam War. More exactly, I was recalling the loss of a large, youthful sense of social hope that the civil rights movement had awakened and that had crashed in the course of the next decade, like a car falling slowly from a high cliff.

Review the film of the loss frame by frame, and you will see the vehicle tumbling through large events: Martin Luther King's death, Robert Kennedy's, Watts, the Chicago convention, My Lai, accompanied by a near infinity of smaller ones: Fred Hampton's murder, the napalmed girl, the nightly body counts on television news, the clubbed and tear-gassed protesters. By the early seventies, there was the Cambodia invasion, the Watergate hearings, Nixon's resignation, finally ending with photos of Vietnamese men desperately grasping the wings and wheel axles of the planes they had hoped would carry them out of Saigon ahead of the conquering North Vietnamese troops. "Ho Ho Ho Chi Minh," we used to chant during the protests, "NLF is gonna win." And finally, when we no longer saw meaning in the event, it did.

The experience of protest was of torment and futility. The hope that began the effort gave way to weary cynicism. Yet read history and you will conclude that anti-war protesters shortened the Vietnam War and saved lives. We changed the world and we would continue to do so. Our lives would be about change, some of it brand new, some of it a legacy inherited almost unexplored from recent generations. As a woman I have the opportunity to manage my money, write this essay, vote, divorce, control my child-bearing, travel alone, choose my partner, and marry across race, class, and religion. I am the beneficiary of efforts by women of my generation, my mother's, and my grandmother's, and can say sincerely that change has been abundant, and that it has constituted progress. So too, the social protest of my own lifetime starting with the civil rights movement, then the Vietnam War, the women's movement and the anti nuclear movement, has yielded many important changes—among them the diminution of racism and sexism, the shortening of an unjust war, and the lowering of the total number of nuclear missiles in the world.

How is it, then, that the result of protest and progress appears to be a widespread silence about the future, a kind of *aw shucks* embarrassment about idealism or visions of social change? I don't think that the mostly middle-class or affluent—largely white—professionals who were once the student war protesters by and large feel a personal hopelessness, or a sense of despair for their own children's actual prospects. Private life is full of possibility for people who control such a large piece of the world's resources. Yet my generation has been almost totally unable to provide ourselves or our children with a horizon on which to focus a collective vision of meaningful social progress or hope.

The teenagers—friends of my sons—who come in and out of our house every day are lively and bright, likely as adults to improve computer technology and protect the ozone. But, as far as I can tell, not one of them would be caught dead dreaming aloud of a better world. Their idealism lacks a shared public language or goal. Not for them a city on a hill, or the uniting of the world's workers. Their youth makes them blind to the struggles that have preceded them. Yet their intuition is like Braille-trained fingers with which they rub their surroundings and perceive that they are the puzzled legatees of others' ambitious dreams, utopian plans, and ideological disappointments. They are not sure what they have inherited, or how to name—beyond more money and things—what they might want.

How do you make dreams of progress for people who—by every historical and conventional measure—have arrived? And recently arrived at that. As opposed to *nouveau riche,* which some might be, the more important but less noticed truth is that many are *nouveau libéré*—newly liberated. Racial prejudice is virulent in America, as are economic and class barriers. But place most people beside their grandparents, and the amount of personal freedom and choice they have is greatly enlarged. More often than not the immigrants who landed here—even those neither indentured nor enslaved— brought little with them, and made what they could with what they found. My neighborhood in a suburb south of Boston is filled with Irish families who live in freshly renovated houses and own new cars. Their grandparents crowded into the Boston tenements, their great grandparents arrived in steerage, forced—as Andrea Barrett reminds us in *Ship Fever*—to abandon the bodies of loved ones who had starved en route. For years during the nineteenth century help-wanted advertisements read "n.i.n.a.": no Irish need apply.

And often this past was not that long ago. The literary phenomenon of 1997 is *Angela's Ashes,* Frank McCourt's memoir of growing up in awful poverty in Ireland in the years before World War II. The book has sold over a million copies in hardcover and is still high on the bestseller list. Just as *Fiddler on the Roof* offered Jewish audiences of the 1960s a narrative that explained how they got to Long Island, *Angela's Ashes* has done the same for the Irish—and both works speak to many Americans. These artistic inventions draw mass audiences because people experience them as prosthetic limbs for pasts amputated by the discontinuity of assimilation and prosperity. People strap them on in place of the real missing stories of earlier old-world generations. They stand in for the personal history that is lost.

Audiences flock to *Angela's Ashes* and *Fiddler on the Roof* seeking reassurance that the present is better. It is comforting to be reminded that the world left behind was often filled with suffering and terrible choices. At the same time, by entering these dramas, people enjoy the restoration of a familiar, delicious, and now lost hope for progress and a better life. (The musical and the memoir both end with emigration. Unencumbered by experience, the characters behold the new land's promise.) Oh, for the days—one can say sentimentally from the safety of plenitude—when people knew what they wanted—when dreams of progress were of food, shelter, freedom, and a large, new world for one's children. Now that the real accompanying terrors are safely in the past, we enjoy revisiting such dreams. Several years ago I watched my son's sixth grade class perform a rousing chorus of "Food, Glorious Food," from the musical *Oliver*. These affluent children delighted in their role as starving orphans in search of better gruel. Nothing relieves the soul like a borrowed wish; particularly since in prosperity we have lost the sufferer's prerogative of earned righteousness about our own desires.

"Ah," Ralph Waldo Emerson once wrote, "if the rich were rich as the poor fancy riches."* We resist the notion that arrival includes mourning the loss of the dream of arrival, but it does. When the poor fancy riches, two imaginative acts occur at once. People dream of real solutions to the economic problems that consume their lives. But the particular hope for money is fused to a wish for escape from the present, and perhaps from the very confines of the psychological self. However much images of the future are set in material terms, at heart they are also fantasies of emotional release. In them, surroundings are altered, and people are, too. One seeks to feel new, to dissolve the restrictions of convention, habit, worn landscape, and familiar love. One dilemma of arrival is that the mind loses—but still insists on—a fantasy of arrival. The real present remains imperfect. Yet once basic needs have been satisfied, the props to fill dreams become more rarefied, elusive, idiosyncratic, and diffuse.

*Ralph Waldo Emerson, *Nature,* VIII Essays: Second Series (Cambridge: Riverside Press, 1903).

Middle-class Americans are—for the moment—sheltered from all the conventional terrors: political oppression, genocide, poverty, starvation, homelessness, and diseases that wipe out half a neighborhood in a day. In such a context, what is progress's rallying cry? History suggests that in time, either from adversity or purpose, new ideas will stir. Gradually, they will ready and lift off. But now the flock—perhaps worn from the last long lap—is consumed in feeding and sleeping, oblivious to larger imperative.

And what of the grief that welled up that night at dinner? I think it had two sources. The first was feeling a long suppressed and carefully denigrated passion for social justice come back unexpectedly. The second was the memory of what a painful era the sixties and early seventies had been. Caring about the direction the world took had turned out to include opening oneself to bad surprises. The poet W. D. Snodgrass describes finding a picture of his first wife in a pile of old papers he is sorting. For him, it is like turning up a severed hand while raking leaves.

I was sixteen when Robert Kennedy was murdered. A young woman teacher at my high school and I, made restless by the proximity of summer, had driven up to camp overnight by the ocean. At dawn we turned on the car radio and heard the news of the assassination as we peered out through dew-covered windows at sand dunes and beach grass. We drove back in a daze of anguish. All weekend I lay in bed with an awful stomachache, and spoke to no one about my grief. I was ashamed to admit I had fallen for the virile, suntanned man in the white shirt with the rolled-up shirtsleeves who drew huge crowds and promised a better world. But the truth was that I believed in the world he was describing, a place freed of racism, poverty, and pointless wars. A place where we could sacrifice personal gain for the sake of social fairness.

To lose someone who in reality has no connection to you, but in fantasy has captured you, is a particular kind of loss. For even as you are pummeled by grief, you never feel fully entitled to your mourning. Rather, you feel embarrassed, caught out caring when you should have known better. What kind of naïve girl were you anyway to admire such a compromised, uneasy man? Or worse, to believe that a different world was possible? To see virtue in voluntary poverty?

But my feelings about Robert Kennedy are important here only insofar as they were emblematic. Our emotional experience during the era was often of an exquisite vulnerability that is as difficult to name, describe, or recapture as it was to live through. By agreeing to care, we opened ourselves to pain. Suffering by choice for causes not obviously our own—the fate of the Vietnamese people, the well-being of the American downtrodden—gradually made us feel mistaken, even foolish.

I had suppressed all this until I read Carroll's memoir. Or more precisely, I had blamed myself for feeling too much, and decided that it was a personal problem. Carroll's book made me weep because it declared that that era's anguish and the participants' grief had been legitimate and widely felt. Like a parent who refuses to enter the room where a beloved child has died, I had tried to shut away the memory of how much we had cared—and how perhaps the best thing about us was that we did. Carroll took me back into that room, and I remembered the child's touch and smell, the overwhelming bond, and what it still held of my own passion.

Vietnam was a bad war, and our protest was enlightened even as it contributed to the anguish, the father-against-son fury, that Carroll describes. The accompanying pursuit of greater social and economic equality was also right. But at the time it felt too hard. Our leaders had been killed. Adulthood was waiting. We put down the placards, returned to graduate school, and found professions. There were children to raise, and mutual funds to worry over. So much was possible. We concentrated on sampling the fruit before us—figs, apricots, tangerines—crates overflowing with worldly delights. And we quietly abandoned our large idealism. Left it, shook it off, took it to the edge of the woods and instructed it not to follow us home. Drowned it in a stream. Held it under the water until we thought it was still. For a while, life seemed better without it.

DEBORAH TANNEN

Connections

My father never knew his father. Until he was seven, he lived with his mother and sister in his grandparents' home: a Hasidic household in Warsaw. His grandfather was the closest he ever came to having a father.

In 1920, when my father was twelve, he left Poland to emigrate with his mother and sister to the United States, and he saw his grandfather for the last time. As my father tells it, his grandfather took him on his knee to say good-bye. Tears ran down the old man's face and into his long white beard. He knew he would never see his grandchild again. Even if the Holocaust had not taken his grandfather's life, my father would not have been able to return to Poland for a visit during his grandfather's lifetime. He wouldn't have been able to take the time off work to sail across the ocean, and he wouldn't have been able to afford the trip.

In 1966, I graduated from college, worked for six months, saved all the money I earned, and flew to Europe on a one-way ticket through Luxembourg on Icelandic Airlines. I ended up in Greece, where I lived for nearly two years, teaching English. I communicated with my parents by mail—but from time to time I would telephone them: I'd go to the main post office in downtown Athens, fill out a form, and wait until someone called my name and indicated in which booth my parents' voices would materialize. Sometimes I waited hours for the call to be put through—until the planned evening surprise had become a terrifying, sleep-destroying, wee-hours-of-the-morning alarm. "Do me a favor," my mother once said. "If it's after midnight, don't call." "But I've been waiting to put the call through for four hours," I said. "I didn't plan it to be after midnight." And there were not only telephones, but airplanes. During that year, my parents celebrated their thirty-fifth wedding anniversary, and they gave each of their children $1000. I used a portion of mine to fly home to New York City for their anniversary party.

In 1996, my oldest sister went to Israel for a year. Within a few weeks, she subscribed to Compuserve and hooked up her laptop computer to e-mail—and my other sister and my nieces all got on e-mail, too. Within a month, my sister was in daily communication with us all—much more frequent contact than our weekly (or biweekly or monthly) telephone calls had been when my sister was home in upstate New York.

And another surprise: my other sister, who generally is not eager to talk about her feelings, opened up on e-mail. One time I called her and we spoke on the phone; after we hung up, I checked my e-mail and found a message she had sent before we spoke, in which she revealed personal information that she hadn't mentioned on the phone. I asked her about this (on e-mail), and she explained, "The telephone is so impersonal." At first this seemed absurd: How could the actual voice of a person in conversation be more impersonal than on-screen little letters detached from the writer? But when I thought about it, it made sense: Writing e-mail is like writing in a journal; you're alone with your thoughts and your words, safe from the intrusive presence of another person.

I was the second person in my university department to get a computer. The first was my colleague Ralph. The year was 1980. Ralph got a Radio Shack TRS 80; I got a used Apple 2-Plus. He helped me get started, and before long helped me get on Bitnet, the precursor to the Internet. Though his office was next to mine, we rarely had extended conversations except about department business. Shy and soft-spoken, Ralph mumbled so, I could barely tell he was speaking. But when we were using e-mail, we started communicating daily in this (then) leisurely medium. We could send each other messages without fear of imposing, since the receiver determines when to log on and read and respond. Soon I was getting long, self-revealing messages from Ralph. We moved effortlessly among discussions of department business, our work, and our lives. Through e-mail Ralph and I became friends.

Ralph recently forwarded to me a message he had received from his niece, a college freshman. "How nice," I commented, "that you have such a close relationship with your niece. Do you think you'd be in touch with her if it weren't for e-mail?" "No," he replied. "I can't imagine we'd write each other letters regularly or call on the phone. No way." E-mail makes possible connections with relatives, acquaintances, or strangers, that wouldn't otherwise exist. And it enables more frequent and different communication with people you're already close to. Parents are in daily contact with their children at college; people discover and reunite with long lost friends. One woman discovered that e-mail brought her closer to her father. He would never talk much on the phone (as her mother would), but they have become close since they both got on-line.

The Internet and the World Wide Web are creating networks of human connection unthinkable even a few years ago. But at the same time that technologically enhanced communication enables previously impossible loving contact, it also enhances hostile and distressing communication. Along with the voices of family members and friends, telephones bring into our homes the annoying voices of solicitors who want to sell something—at dinnertime. (My father-in-law startles a telephone solicitor by saying, "We're eating dinner, but I'll call you back. What's your home phone number?" To the nonplussed caller he explains, "Well, you're calling me at home; I thought I'd call you at home, too.") Even more unnerving, in the middle of the night come frightening obscene calls and stalkers.

The Internet ratchets up anonymity by homogenizing all messages into identical-appearing print and making it almost impossible to trace messages back to the computer that sent them. As the ease of using the Internet has resulted in more and more people logging on and sending messages to more and more others with whom they have a connection, it has also led to more communication with strangers, and this has led to "flaming": vituperative messages that verbally attack. Flaming results from the anonymity not only of the sender but also of the receiver. It is easier to feel and express hostility against someone far removed whom you do not know, like the rage that some drivers feel toward an anonymous car that cuts them off. If the driver to whom you've flipped the finger turns out to be someone you know, the rush of shame you feel is evidence that anonymity was essential for your expression—and experience—of rage.

Less and less of our communication is face to face, and more often with people we don't know. Technology that brings people closer also isolates us in a bubble. When I was a child, my family got the first television on our block, and the neighborhood children gathered in our dining room to watch *Howdy Doody*. Before long, every family had their own TV—just one, so that in order to watch it, families came together. Now many families have more than one television, so each family member can watch what they like—alone. The spread of radio has followed the same pattern. Early radios were like a piece of furniture around which a family had to gather in order to listen. Now radio listeners may have a radio in every room, one in the car, and another—equipped with headphones—for jogging. These technologies now exert a centrifugal force, pulling people apart—and increasing the likelihood that their encounters with each other will be anonymous and hostile.

Electronic communication is progress; it makes human relationships different. But it also makes human relationships more the same—there's more of what's good and more of what's bad. In the end, we graft the new possibilities onto what has always been there.

E-mail gave me the chance to be in touch with someone who was dying far away. College friends, Larry and I were not so close that we would make special trips to visit each other on opposite coasts, but we kept in touch through occasional notes, and we got together whenever we found ourselves in the same town. I learned from another college friend—on e-mail—that Larry was diagnosed with lung cancer. I didn't want to call Larry on the phone; that seemed too intrusive. I didn't know if he wanted to talk about his cancer with people like me; maybe he wanted to curl into his family. So I sent him an e-mail message, and he sent one in reply. Soon we were exchanging messages regularly. E-mail gave me a little path I could walk along. For two years, Larry kept me informed of how he was doing, and what the chemotherapy was doing to him—and asked me how my book was coming and whether I had managed to put up pictures in my new house yet. In April 1996 he was back to work and gaining weight. But then e-mail brought the bad news: new lesions were found, and the doctors held out no more hope.

On December 24, 1996, Larry wrote, "I will miss our e-mails, Deb. It was great being your friend, and I will always remain so." On December 27 I got messages—both on e-mail and on my telephone answering machine—telling me Larry had died the night before. I could not just sit at my desk that day and work. And e-mail was not immediate enough for the connection I wanted. I called friends who had been closer to Larry than I, to learn as much as I could about his last days. And I called friends who had been less close, to tell them. I spent much of that day talking with friends from our college circle. We told each other our memories of Larry's life, creating our own memorial to observe his passing from our lives.

My father never knew exactly when his grandfather died. When my friend Larry died, how much it meant that the telephone made it possible to spend the day talking to others who knew him. How much it meant that Larry said good-bye. This is a gift he gave me, and technology made it possible. That is progress. But the way we used technology—the telephone and e-mail—that was human emotion and experience as old as time.

REBECCA WALKER

Progress and Desire

We live at a time in which the Darwinian notion of linear progress—of moving in some logical manner toward some perfect
Aryan tomorrow—has been debunked as a myth, yet another device
employed by white European males at the onset of patriarchy to convince people that the obliteration of the Goddess, or the reign of
chaos, or the reign of living peaceably and humbly on the earth, was
in actuality a good thing, the triumph of one superior worldview
over an infinitely flawed and outdated set of "primitive" beliefs.
Feminists, multiculturalists, Luddites, physicists, mystics, and just
ordinary people like you and me who sometimes prefer water to Diet
Coke, a starry night to canned sitcom laughter, have by now raised
enough doubts about the positivism of colonialism, the biological
mandate of inequality, the benevolence of technology, and the democracy inherent in consumerism and free trade. We know, even if
we lack some wholly coherent alternative, that "progress," as cham-
pioned by politicians, pharmaceutical companies, and investment
bankers alike, often leaves us sorely wanting; that progress may not,
in fact, make our lives better than they were before.

This is not to say that important gains and significant advances
too numerous to list here, both in civil matters and scientific discovery, have not been made. But because of our exposure to the great
diversity that comprises our earth's population, we are now aware

that one group or individual's working definition of stunning, life-affirming progress may be another's definition of death and demise, and yet another's portrait of ego-preserving denial and spiritual depravity. What perplexes is that still, even amidst all of this rampant deconstruction, this archetypal trope called progress, this underlying need to write our story always with the promise of a better day ahead (nirvana, heaven, romantic love, material success) persists. Even as we acknowledge its glaring impossibility, the idea of progress continues to seduce and ensnare us.

Buddhists believe, and I agree, that humans are addicted to this thing we call progress because at any given moment in our lifetimes one thousand desires are swimming around in our various psyches and we, such beautiful and pathetic slaves to desire, chase around after these desires, naming our growing proximity to said desires "progress." I'm not just talking about your desire to be rich, or for your next-door neighbor to be injected with a dose of humility, or to find the perfect mate. The desires we chase, the wants that ultimately define progress for us can be, and usually are (for we are a species with a huge propensity for drama) grand.

We desire world peace, the eradication of human suffering, an end to the exploitation of animals and the earth. We desire a world without disease, without hypocrisy, without persecution based on race, gender, class, religion, or culture. Or we desire a world in which our group or community is primary, superior, dominant over all the rest. We desire the end of this planet and the colonization of others, we desire the supremacy of technology over humanity, the submission of the majority to the minority, of the moneyed with their cell phones and video games and plane tickets to the poor, with their two-mile walks for clean water and their unceasing toil. The narrative of progress to which one ascribes is shaped by a great many random factors such as how much money you make and how you make it, what your parents believed and your subsequent relationship to them, what books you have read, and what pain or joy you have experienced and at what cost.

Progress then is not a simple ideal but an infinitely complicated project, with desire at its root. And we all know how fickle and unruly, how demanding and unquenchable desire can be. Desire comes, for better or for worse, from a particular dis-ease with the way things are; desire comes from not being content with what you have or who you are, desire comes from wanting More, Other, Not This. While this wanting can fuel the greatest of revolutions, it can also, if it burns unchecked, become a perpetual state of being. In this manifestation, there is always something else to set your sights on, something else out there to fill the incessant craving. If a person or, let's say, a nation, grows addicted to fulfilling its desires, to constantly making "progress," it can be quite difficult for that person or nation to enjoy the fruits of their last achievement. The person or nation is unable to rest in a state of satiation, to define or understand itself based on what it has or what it, in essence, is. It is always defined by what it lacks, what is missing, what is yet to be attained.

When I was in junior high school, I desired that a white hockey player named Greg Battalia would fall in love with me, that a Dominican boy named James Collado would too, and that I, a light-skinned biracial girl living in New York, would suddenly find some world outside of my body that would accept me as I was, without having to straighten my hair or speak solely in Ebonics, or betray myself in any number of other ways. When I reached high school, a white man fell in love with me and then a black one did too, and instead of searching for that perfect community, I retreated into the worlds of books and movies and their infinite variety of experience. I desired my driver's license, and to go to a good college, and to do "important" political work on behalf of women and people of color. Now I have driven across the country, and graduated "with honors" from an Ivy League school, and started an organization for young women's activism, and yet I find myself here again, at the wanting hole, measuring myself and my value by how closely my external life approximates my personal progress narrative. Does my body finally have a caption overhead which reads "Happy," "Successful," "Arrived," or "Fulfilled"?

Honestly, I feel the same as I did in junior high. I am the same young woman looking for love, home, and security, the same young woman who wants to exist whole, without cutting off any parts. Now I desire to write a book, to settle down with the person I love, but I question the whole notion of desire, the whole notion of progress. Certainly as I work on my book, each day yields another page or paragraph, and I inch closer to having a finished product, an external measure of time and distance mastered. Yet when I sit to write, as I hover around the ideas in my mind I am still filled with the same insecurities, the same feelings of dread and excitement. As I move closer to my lover and our bond is strengthened, I dare to believe we too are making progress, building trust, getting closer to fulfilling this want. Yet I am filled with the same fears and trepidations; the same specters of betrayal and possible loss still haunt me. Will my desires ever cease? Will I never be at peace?

The many "special interest groups" that comprise America also chase after symbols of progress, tangible manifestations of desires attained: cloned sheep, the cure for AIDS, the preservation of the spotted owl, welfare reform, an increased minimum wage, the destruction of nuclear warheads, an abortion pill. Whether or not we agree on which things can rightly be called progress is neither the point nor my question; whether or not there is any end in sight to the remedies we need, to the outcomes we desire, is. How does knowing that desires are endless, and that "progress" as a national mandate is undefinable, alter our perception of what we do everyday, of who we are? What happens if we accept that the utopia we dream about, whether filled with peace or total destruction, may never come to be; that the goal we have rooted so firmly in our little minds will, in all likelihood, elude us?

Fresh from studying political philosophy at Oxford as a Rhodes Scholar, a good friend tells me that even though both of his parents were in the civil rights movement and he spends all of his time running an organization devoted to meeting the basic needs of American children, he thinks that really, there is no such thing as progress. Basically, he says, very matter-of-fact from a cell phone in a cab speeding to take him to see his biracial girlfriend run in the Olympics, all through time, in every era, there has been horror: famine,

torture, persecution, slavery, genocide. There are always good people
and bad people, there are always people who are oppressed and
people who are oppressing, and each are always in some state of doing good or doing ill. What changes, he says, is simply who these
people are and where they live. From era to era the geographical loca-
tions shift, the specific demographics, but nothing else. The basic ratio of good to evil always stays the same.

After we hang up, I am filled with questions; his prognosis seems
so bleak. What about the gradual collective ascendance of human
consciousness? What about the project of reclaiming the subjectivity
of oppressed peoples, in the hopes that the oppressor will be unable
to recognize the oppressed as separate from him or herself and thus
will be unable to continue oppressing? Can there truly be no end in
sight to dualism, to good and evil? And where is hope, that other
great human emotion that fuels progress? Has my friend so dead-
ened his heart that he no longer feels hopeful? For a while I sit, disturbed, staring at the phone.

But I sense a not too subtle mirroring going on here. Though I
am somewhat repulsed by his philosophy, and sorely tempted to dis-
miss his words as yet another plot of higher education to rob students
of their nascent sense of personal power, I feel that my friend is telling me what I already, intuitively, know. For how else would I be able
to forge ahead knowing that I may never reach the place of full satisfaction? How else would I be able to tackle another essay knowing
that no matter how pleased I am with it, when it is time to start another I will feel the same dread I thought I had overcome? The fact is
that I do not truly enter my best work—political, literary, or psychological—until I, too, gently extricate whatever is before me from the
grand narratives of progress and desire. Whether at a rally, in a meeting, or working on a chapter in my book, I delve more deeply and
take greater risks when I avoid fixating on the jewel that may or may
not be hewn from the proverbial rock. Relationships grow stronger,
unforeseen resolutions miraculously emerge, and paragraphs magi-
cally unfurl. Ironically, I make the most progress when I am not concerned with making progress.

Instead of making me complacent or lazy, this freedom from the dogged march of progress gives me more energy for the work to be done; I feel less like the future of humankind is on my shoulders, and more like I can actually manage the infintesimally small part that is mine alone. Liberated, I am free to be present where I am; I can explore knowing that in the larger scheme of things I have already arrived. My friend is right in the wonderfully pragmatic way he is often right: there will be no magic solution, no pinnacle of perfection to achieve after which we can all go inside and lie down. The key is to go on doing what you do, believing in it day by day and step by step. Desire can motivate the journey, but should not define it. Hope is blissfully unaware of the future. Attached but not attached to the outcome, we are free not always to enjoy, but at least to experience, the realm of the process.

Which, anyway, is all there is.

SHAWN WONG

"The Chinese Man Has My Ticket"

After President Nixon traveled to China in the early seventies, my friends kept asking me when I would visit China, the country of my ancestry. I was born in America and have never been to China. Over the years, the question of going has changed to a presumption, "Of course you've been there." Upon learning that I'm Chinese, strangers will describe their trip to China. Sometimes I let them assume that I've already seen what they describe. I nod with comprehension and even say, "Ah, yes." I feel guilty because these well-meaning people want to tell their stories to one who knows. I'm Chinese after all. "Been there, done that" should be my answer.

To complicate matters, I also tell people that I teach Asian American literature, which most people take to mean something from the Tang dynasty, rather than literature written in America by Americans of Asian ancestry. Sometimes I'm asked if the literature is translated, to which I usually respond, "Not yet." In my literature classes, most of the students are Asian, but even I have to look in my pronunciation guide to Asian names before the first day of class. When I was an undergraduate at Berkeley, Asian students accounted for only 6 percent of the student body and we were predominantly middle-class Chinese and Japanese Americans, born and raised in America. Today, on a large campus like Berkeley or the University of Washington, there might be 12 to 15 different Asian ethnic groups plus Asian students of mixed racial heritage, and they might account for 20 to 40 percent of the student body. In an attempt to remember my students' names on the first day of class, I write down who they look like next to their names—actors, musicians, friends, or former students. It doesn't do any good to write "black hair, brown eyes, glasses." Even the term *Asian American* is being contested by this new population. They want to know what it means and why my college generation from the late sixties named ourselves Asian Americans.

In the seventies, I tried to get my aunt to take me to China to find my roots and to show me where our family had lived. I saw it as an act of self-determination. A staunch anti-Communist, my aunt refused to go, saying, "I want to remember it the way it was." Aunt Ching-yi first arrived in America in 1938 when she came as a graduate student to attend Mills College, and she has never returned to China.

My parents arrived in America from China fifty years ago on October 31, 1947. My father and my aunt's younger brother, Peter Hsu, was thirty and my mother, Maria, was twenty-two. Like my aunt, they entered America with student visas. They were not poor immigrants. My father was a graduate student in civil engineering at the University of California at Berkeley and my mother was an art student at the California College of Arts and Crafts. Like my aunt, they were well educated; they could read, write, and speak English. They came from relatively wealthy families. My mother was a painter, photographer, dancer, and musician. She didn't know how to cook or even boil water. My father was an engineer who wrote beautiful letters and stories in English. In China, he was an award-winning athlete. He was tall, six-foot-two, and handsome; she was petite and truly beautiful. After the Communists took over China in 1949, they were granted permanent residency in America, the same year I was born in Oakland, California. With an American-born son, they realized that America was their home and there was no return to China. They never insisted that I learn Chinese. They were learning to be Americans; why would they teach me to be Chinese? My father wore double-breasted suits and drove a Buick Roadmaster, and my mother wore cashmere sweaters, silk scarves, and wool skirts. We went to Cal football games. They never did return to China; they both died here in America. I was supposed to be the best American son I could be, not to be Chinese. Assimilation and acculturation in the fifties were pervasive for all immigrants in America, the melting pot.

I've been to Hong Kong three times and to Japan once as a child, and to Hong Kong for a week to visit my grandmother when I was twenty-one, which was twenty-seven years ago. The irony is that my grandmother visited us in America every year rather than the other way around, then later moved to America. In 1996, she died at the age of ninety-nine in San Francisco. I lived in Taiwan for six months when I was seven and on the island of Guam for a year when I was six. I always felt out of place as an English-speaking Chinese kid in Hong Kong and Taiwan. During one of our longer stays, my mother dropped me off at a preschool in Hong Kong, but I came home after the first day and told my mother that I quit school because I couldn't understand anyone, because all the kids spoke Chinese. All this travel back and forth across the Pacific was the result of my father's work as a civilian engineer for the U.S. Navy. My mother has a picture of me dressed in full leather cowboy chaps and vest with hat and six guns standing in front of the Grand Hotel in Taipei, Taiwan. I remember singing "Home on the Range." In Taiwan, I was the only Chinese kid in an all-white American school. If there was ever a perfect time for an identity crisis, that was it.

I've never been comfortable in Asian countries. My face makes people assume that I belong. They speak their native tongues to me, expecting an answer. They are unwilling to believe that I'm a monolingual American, educated in a monolingual and monocultural public school system. When I was twenty-one I visited my grandmother in Hong Kong. Everyone on the street spoke Cantonese to me. I told them that I didn't speak Cantonese. To make matters worse, they then asked me in Mandarin if I spoke Mandarin. I can understand Mandarin, because my parents spoke Mandarin, but I can't speak it. When I was growing up my parents would often speak to me in Mandarin and I would answer in English. To the people in Hong Kong, I'm stupid because I don't know my own mother tongue, or worse, refuse to speak it. There's a word for Chinese like me: *jook sing,* "hollow bamboo." It means that we look Chinese, but are hollow and lack cultural substance on the inside. Sixty percent of the Asians in America are foreign born, which makes me the exception rather than rule in the country of my birth. People in Asia know I'm foreign and people in America assume that I am foreign born. Sometimes I am asked how long I've been in this country; I always answer my age. Not getting the joke, some people have even replied, "No wonder I didn't hear an accent in your voice."

Like my father, my work defines my travel. So far I've been in every region of the United States from Hawaii and Alaska to Texas, North Carolina, and Florida, and in Europe to the United Kingdom, Ireland, Germany, France, and Italy. Ironically, my writing life is linked more to Germany and Italy than to any other country. My two novels have been translated and published in Germany and some of my short stories have been translated and published in Italy, but in no Asian countries, even though my books are about Asian America. I can read and speak German and some Italian. I am more comfortable in Italy than in any foreign country. Call it the revenge of Marco Polo.

I wrote my second novel, *American Knees,* while on a Rockefeller Foundation residency in Bellagio, northern Italy, in 1994. The novel is set, for the most part, in San Francisco's Asian American community. The dry cleaner in the little village of Bellagio didn't take my name when I left my clothes; she wrote *"cinese"* on a little tag and pinned it to my clothes. I was pleased that she at least got my ethnicity right. Sometimes being the only Asian for miles around is an advantage. In the afternoons, I learned to play bocce ball and the residents of Bellagio would take it upon themselves to teach me Italian.

One day, tired of speaking Italian poorly, I walked down the hill to visit two dogs in the village, one a brown-and-white boxer who lived at the *gelateria* and the other a light brown cocker spaniel from the photo store. Whenever I petted one, the other competed for my affection. I knew they would always understand me. Later, I bought postcards from the man who owns the photo store and I said to him, *"Bella cane,* beautiful dog." That's the way I speak Italian. Having learned from phrase books and tapes, I say the whole phrase and the translation as if those I'm speaking to can't understand their own language. At other times I say, "*Va bene,* OK." Sometimes the Italians are drawn into my way of speaking and answer, "*Arrivederci,* good-bye." A little more of that dialogue and we'd be singing the Italian version of a Nat King Cole song sung in French.

By my third trip to Italy in 1997, I developed an uncanny fluency in all matters relating to Italian food, restaurants, markets, and public transportation. I also understand numbers, time, directions, weights, and measures. I am far more polite in Italian than I am in English. I am uncomfortable not knowing the language when I'm in Italy, but, unlike in Asia, no one expects me to know it. I feel helpless and stupid, because I feel like the monolingual American that I am. The owner of the grocery store in Rome where I shopped declared one day that he wasn't going to speak English to me any more and that I must speak Italian from then on. "I am going to give you character," he told me. "I'm going to teach you past tense—you only know present tense." I was immensely grateful to this wonderful man, who spoke five languages.

Generally, people in Europe are more than happy to speak English to me, because they don't think I'm an American. They think I'm a Japanese tourist. I know zero French and what French I do know, I dare not even pretend to pronounce, so I speak English to everyone. In Paris, everyone is very polite, unlike the stories Americans tell about rude Parisians who refuse to speak English. Most Parisians are relieved that I speak English so well. At Charles de Gaulle Airport, I'm directed to the flights to Tokyo before I ask about my flight to Chicago.

Whenever I'm in Europe I'm always curious as to whether or not I can discern the difference between mild racism and cultural confusion. In Rome, when people are rude to me, I try to figure out if they're being rude because I'm Asian, or American, or a Japanese tourist. This is very confusing for someone who, at home in America, can easily recognize a racist comment. In Europe I don't know if I need to stand up for my race or my country or my self-respect as a cash-spending tourist.

In the summer of 1997, I took fourteen of my University of Washington students, nine graduates and five undergraduates, to Rome for a month-long creative writing course, designed to reshape their thinking outside of the familiarity of their culture and language. We made a curious-looking group on the streets of Rome. Picture this: one Chinese American professor, twelve white women, one *hapa* (half-Asian woman), and one Chinese American male student. Prior to taking my students to Rome, I had only spent three days there in 1994, and probably knew of Rome no more than Audrey Hepburn did in the movie *Roman Holiday* (and I was no Gregory Peck). To say this was an experiment would be a gross understatement. It had the potential for gross chaos or fabulous discovery for all of us. This seemed like a good way to celebrate my twenty-fifth year of teaching. Why Rome?

How does one prepare for the twenty-first century? I tell my students to acknowledge the diversity of culture and language in this country and the world. I wanted to take my students and, more importantly, myself, out of our realm of cultural familiarity. Only then can we go forward and make real progress. "Let's get out of the classroom," I said to them. "You're writers."

My own writing has changed dramatically every time I've been away from my country. It was time to practice what I preached in the classroom about our responsibility to learn about other cultures. I wanted my students not only to write about Rome, but also to observe and document images that are completely foreign to their experience. I wanted them to also observe, in intricate detail, things that could be used in their writing even when it wasn't about Rome. Describe the light. Describe the interior space of the Pantheon. Learn the jargon of architecture. Examine the space and the quality of the light between buildings. Immerse ourselves in the images of antiquity and religion, the culture of contemporary Rome, the history of Italian art, and the language. Walk the Via Appia Antica, the ancient Roman road.

Outside of Rome, I took them to Tivoli to see the opulence of the Villa d'Este and to the sprawling expanse of the ruins of Hadrian's Villa; to Tarquinia to visit the Etruscan tombs where we gazed up from the pages of D. H. Lawrence's *Etruscan Places* and matched his words to the tombs we visited; to the dead city of Pompeii and to the luxurious vacation town of Sorrento where my students swam in the Gulf of Naples; and to the medieval hilltowns of Orvieto and Civita di Bagnoregio, the latter a magical town of the imagination, an Etruscan fortress perched on a rock and reachable only by footbridge. In Rome we saw everything from the underground necropolis of the Vatican, to the cloister of tiny Santi Quattro Coronati, to the bejeweled *il Bambino,* the Holy Infant of Aracoeli, to nearly every Caravaggio painting accessible to the public. Each day we bought food from the vendors in the Campo de' Fiori and cooked fabulous late evening dinners. My students taught themselves and taught me. On public transportation and entering museums my students had taught themselves this mantra without telling me, *"L'uomo cinese ha il mio biglietto."* The Chinese man has my ticket. Train conductors accepted this explanation even though my students and I were sometimes separated by several crowded train cars while I held the only group ticket. I love them for their fearlessness, their adaptability, their acculturation, and their appetite for being a part of the world.

I believe we were all changed forever by the experience. After Rome, I returned home and nearly all of my students scattered across Italy and Europe to Siena, Florence, Venice, Milan, Prague, Paris, London, Dublin, Vienna, Barcelona, Jerusalem, and Istanbul. Not only did they all come home, but they came home with stories written with words I'd never seen on their pages before.

When I came home, my eighty-four-year-old aunt sent me an e-mail telling me that she had been writing her memoirs of her life in China and America. Since I'm the writer in the family, she wanted me to help her with her memoirs, over three hundred pages long. I was behind on my own writing projects, and meeting with her would involve flying from my home in Seattle to San Francisco, so all I could manage was a politely filial reply, "Sure, I'd be happy to look at it." She mailed it to me, along with her diaries, letters, and notes. Her three-hundred-page story begins with the following paragraph:

When I was sixteen, my father fell in love with a prostitute and brought her home to live with us. Her name was Hsin Pao. We all hated her intensely, but she was only two years older than I and we had a lot to talk about. My study became her room. My brother called me "traitor." My mother eventually accepted her and was even glad to have someone to play mahjongg with. Sometime later, my father took Hsin Pao to Tientsin to meet my father's other wife and family.

In Rome, I wanted my students to be prepared for the future, the multicultural world of the twenty-first century. Let's live in the world and move forward. That same month, my aunt was finally taking me into the past on that journey which has become our "return" to China. Self-determination is knowing the past as well as preparing for the future. My aunt tells me that, as a child, she once saw a book that documented sixty-four generations of our family. *Mama mia,* what a marvelous story she tells about the history of our family.

SUSAN WOOD

The Tornado in the Carpet

A month or so before the end of my four-and-a-half-year, four-day-a-week psychoanalysis, I have a dream which I will come to think of as a dream about progress, though progress of a very different sort from what I would once have expected.

In this dream I appear to be much younger than I am and newly married, though not to the man I actually married long ago when I was twenty-one—waking, I can't recall the dream husband's face. He and I have been apartment hunting, it seems, for days, maybe weeks, and have at last found something that we can afford and that both of us like. A dim scene of a room with pale yellow walls, high-ceilings, full of light. But there's one problem: the carpet, I tell him, is "the ugliest carpet I've ever seen!" At that, we both burst into laughter. "Do you think we can tolerate it?" he asks. "Yes," I answer, "I think we can." The carpet is indeed hideous: a rather muddy gray background with what at first appear to be black or darker gray stripes running through it; but they are not stripes in the usual sense—instead, the vertical patterns have a kind of spiral shape.

When I describe it to my analyst, she asks me what the pattern brings to mind. "A tornado," I say without hesitation, though of course I have not known it until now.

In the silence that follows, I lie on the dark green couch and watch the summer afternoon's inevitable rain run down the glass, listen to it fall softly on the leaves of the banana tree in the atrium. I have grown accustomed to the changing weather of this view, the play of sunlight on the peach-colored walls, of sunlight and of rain on the dense greenery outside, so that now, so late in the analysis, it seems like a forest glen, a haven—though, like a small child who hates change, I hated it when the analyst had moved to this fancy new office two years ago. I like it now especially when it rains. The room grows darker, quieter somehow, and she and I are there together, suspended in our private place. I want it to last forever. This room. This womb.

"What are you thinking?" she asks from her chair behind me. I can't see, but imagine, her face. "Tornadoes," I say again.

I've dreamed of them before. Once, maybe two years earlier, I stood on a very high hill, purple with heather, and saw a tornado coming towards me. I was carrying a child and trying to run, but the child was so heavy I could barely move. Suddenly the tornado turned into a purple skeleton grinning hideously in the air above me, a figure in a child's nightmare, and the dream dissolved.

Not long before I had the dream about the carpet, I recalled a dream from years before. When I first remembered it, I thought it had really happened because it seemed so vivid, brought back so hauntingly the years of conflict and divorce, of separation from my children. In it, I'm driving with my small son to visit my parents when, deep in east Texas on an isolated road, I see a twister's black tail dip out of the sky. Terrified, I stop the car and carry my son into a nearby ditch where I lie on top of him, waiting. The dream ends there: I am left in terror, waiting, for what I'm certain will kill us, out there in the open, unprotected.

Tornadoes were part of the actual weather of my childhood in northeast Texas, just south of the Oklahoma border: Tornado Alley. But the truth is, I don't recall ever seeing one, though every black cloud became a portent. If it thundered at night, I would cower beneath the covers, no matter how hot the evening, and hold my breath, waiting for the town siren to announce the twister's imminent approach. It never occurred to me to do anything but wait silently for it, never occurred to me to cry out for my parents—denials or refusals which would be much analyzed—and I passed many sleepless nights like this.

It's clear to me now that this excessive fear was a cover for something else, of course. For the storm beneath the placid surface of the family. For the storm inside of me. For something which could only be uncovered in analysis, something so complex and deep it has no name, is not a single entity.

But by the end of analysis—*termination,* a word with the sound of a steel door in it, I used to think—the tornado appeared in my dream not as a symbol of death but as a pattern in a carpet, a pattern that seemed to represent life, the ordinary conflict and turmoil of life. Not only that, its ugliness was no longer menacing, but a source of amusement. Together the person I loved and I could "tolerate" it.

In any intimate relationship, my analyst reminded me, turmoil is inevitable. "That's something you've always been really reluctant to allow into a relationship," she said. "It's important for you to know not just that it's inevitable, but that you can live with it."

And there was something else I noticed about that carpet. Intellectually, I believed in complexity, knew that things were rarely either black or white, but I often behaved as if I believed they were, a contradiction my analyst had frequently pointed out to me. It was an absolutism learned in my conservative Christian family, where there was one way to feel, to believe, to behave, and it made it difficult for me to acknowledge difference and ambivalent feelings. The background of the carpet in the dream, though, was drawn in shades of gray.

Notice that I have switched to the past tense, that I can now stand to speak of my analysis as having happened in the past. Notice, though, that I call her "the analyst," as if to keep her at a distance. Do I think that I won't feel her loss that way, that I will miss her any less? Her name is Dr. Cole. Letha Cole.

Perhaps in writing this essay, I am trying to deal with—ease by thinking about and talking about—my feelings about the end of my analysis. Three months later I feel both a sense of pleasure and achievement in the changes that resulted from psychoanalysis and a deep grief at the loss of Dr. Cole and our intensely intimate relationship. Sometimes the grief still washes over me suddenly, painfully, but that has begun to happen, I see with some regret, less frequently.

As the psychoanalytic theorist Stephen Mitchell observes, "Analysis does not work unless both analysand and analyst are passionate about the work. Yet this passion, like most passions, has a tragic underside. A passionate analysis, if it is to be maximally effective, must contain an awareness of the limits of the process and the necessary omissions and constraints. . . ." It's the way loving anyone contains within it potential, inevitable loss. Of course it's not just *any* relationship we're talking about, but the one between analyst and analysand, which is unique and must seem strange to those who haven't experienced it. "In that sense," Mitchell says, "termination does not suggest a 'completeness' of the analysis but a readiness to move past the limitations and inevitable incompleteness of the current one." It suggests hope for the future.

When I entered analysis in the spring of 1993, I went, as most people do, because I was not enjoying my life, though really, if I'm honest, it felt more urgent than that. It was more than being "unhappy" or "depressed." I had a vague feeling of being without a center or a self, that there was an open space in my chest where the wind blew through, a draught, an absence, like a ghost, and yet sometimes that place felt heavy, or hard, as if something there needed to be cracked open. For a while I had been plagued by dreams in which my head was severed from my body, a graphic illustration of the rupture between my mind and body, or ones in which I was, quite literally, struggling with my "self," a double, a mirror image. (Once "I" pushed "her" down the stairs.) And over the past twelve or thirteen years, I knew of four or five instances of sleepwalking, a couple of which involved my going outside the places I was living. Though no harm had come to me that way, I was scared that it would. (Sleepwalking, I now see, was an apt metaphor for the way I was stumbling through life, trying not to see or feel.) I had been unable to form any kind of stable, satisfying romantic relationship, and I was having longer and longer periods of writer's block. In short, I was a mess, though on the surface I was still the competent, self-assured poet and professor.

I had been in psychotherapy for relatively brief periods of time twice before, and while both experiences had been immediately helpful, it seemed to me that something more radical, more long lasting was needed. I had been interested in psychoanalysis for years, ever since a graduate course in psychoanalytic approaches to literary criticism, and I had friends who were patients and friends who were analysts. I had read some of the literature—Freud and his explainer, Finichel, and a few of the more contemporary object relations theorists—and was aware of the ways in which psychoanalytic theory and practice have changed since Freud. Though it has retained versions of many of Freud's most important concepts—the unconscious, transference, defense mechanisms, for example—contemporary psychoanalysis has tended to move away from Freud's drive-based theory with its concepts of penis envy, castration complex, oral and anal stages, and the Oedipus complex to theories that explore concepts of the self in its relation to others and sometimes focus on the infant's relationship with the mother and the ways in which disturbances in that relationship are repeated in later ones. To simplify, one could say that psychoanalysis has evolved from an analysis of symptoms, and treatment of them—as in the case of the hysterics, many with serious psychosomatic symptoms, that Freud saw in his consulting room—to the analysis of character, an attempt to treat the individual character in its totality, a treatment for persons who have problems not only with symptoms but with human relationships and the way they conduct their lives, the way they experience pleasure, the ways they approach relationships with others, their careers, and themselves.

Is this progress? Certainly some would argue that this shift toward self psychology and character analysis reflects the primacy of the self in contemporary Western culture and that this is the culture's deep sickness rather than its treatment. (And some would actually blame Freud himself for this, as though without him there would be no concept of the self at all.) On the other hand, one could say that the kinds of pervasive character problems from which people seem to suffer today merely reflect the increasingly mechanistic, fragmented nature of modern life and that whatever eases this suffering is a good thing. It seems important to note that, as I have defined psychoanalysis's interests, it is not geared to making people more narcissistic but less so, by focusing on the individual's relationships with others.

And, in any event, we cannot now turn back the clock, no matter how much some conservative politicians and some religious leaders would like us to. As the world has gotten more complicated, so have the diagnoses and the treatments for emotional problems and mental illnesses. Along with psychoanalysis and psychoanalytic psychotherapy, other short-term cognitive and behavioral therapies have developed to deal with problems like phobias or anxiety, for example. And, of course, more and more, there are drug-based therapies to deal with illnesses like major depression, manic depression, schizophrenia, and obsessive compulsive disorder.

Psychoanalysis is not for everyone, but for someone like me, who was not psychotic, not severely depressed but suffered from a mild, chronic dysthymia, did not have character problems that severely disturbed my ability to function but instead was not enjoying life, not having the kinds of intimate relations with others that I wanted, was not being as productive in any way as I felt I could be, psychoanalysis seemed ideal. An antidepressant might make me feel better but it wouldn't treat what was causing my problems.

Why psychoanalysis, and its founder in particular, are so maligned today seems to me to be another essay—many of its most vociferous critics (and their vociferousness itself is something to be analyzed) do not, I suspect, have much acquaintance with clinical psychoanalysis (as opposed to theoretical) and with what actually goes on in any analytic session, but I did not have to be convinced. I had seen what psychoanalysis had done for others and I hoped it could do the same for me. And it was a given to me that childhood experience shapes our adult behavior and that there is such a thing as the unconscious—mental processes of which we are not consciously aware. (As a friend of mine once said to someone who said he didn't believe in the unconscious, "The unconscious believes in you.")

But could psychoanalysis help me to know my unconscious better, the way you get to know a person better? And what would happen if I did? Would my life be better? Sandor Ferenczi, Freud's early collaborator, with whom Freud fell out in part, interestingly enough, over the issue of how one treats one's patients, put it this way: "Is it possible (?) *to make friends* with the unconscious?" If you could, I wondered, would it want to tell you all its secrets? And would you want to hear them?

More particularly, the fact that psychoanalysis is a lengthy process and that, in some descriptions anyway, it aims at nothing less than a reordering of the psyche seemed somehow hopeful: that what was so deeply rooted in the past would take time and hard work to change made sense to me. Of course, I wanted to be "cured," though what I wanted to be cured of is not quite so clear. To me, cure implies the removal of something, of disease, a "bad thing" growing in the brain, but what I told myself I wanted felt like an addition of something: more wholeness, more completeness, more authenticity. What I really wanted was to "know" and what I wanted to know (and therefore to control) was everything. I wanted all problems solved, all conflict ended, a state which sounds to me now as static as death.

I remember the first time I went to Dr. Cole's office, which was located for the first two years of my analysis in a child development center (fittingly, it seems to me when I think of the child I still was in my mid-forties). A psychiatrist who treated both children and adults, she was then completing further training in order to be qualified as psychoanalyst and I was one of her first analytic patients. The office was plain and slightly disheveled, the couch not a proper analyst's couch but a rather worn sofa covered in a paisley print. The doctor herself, a red-haired woman a few years younger than I, seemed pleasant but reserved. Nothing particularly stuck out about her and yet I felt drawn to her. In retrospect, I think there were things about that room that hinted at passion and humor: on the wall a large Georgia O'Keefe poster of an oversized red, very sexual flower; a bookcase full of psychiatric texts but decorated with a rubber alligator and a green plastic snake; in a corner a dollhouse, a few children's toys, and a little blackboard on which a child had drawn a smiling likeness of Dr. Cole, chin-length bob, glasses, and all.

In any case, I was ready for the transference—the unconscious recreation and repetition of earlier family relationships—to begin. And she, of course, was ready to allow it. ("It is integral to the practice of psychoanalysis," writes the British analyst Adam Phillips, "that the analyst has to fall into the trap of being treated like a parent—an authority of sorts—and then refuse to be one.") From the beginning I knew, though I couldn't articulate it, that I would have to give myself over to the process, to trust her, to dissolve the hard rock that sat in my chest on top of my heart, and that it would be a struggle. Sometimes the few inches of space between the couch and her black leather chair seemed like an ocean, but it was as though she had thrown me a lifeline and I held on with a fierce, even desperate, attachment.

In the weeks and months and years that followed, I lay on that couch and told my story, my stories, over and over, from different angles and different depths while she sat behind me in her black leather chair, her feet resting on an ottoman beside my head, writing in a red spiral notebook. Listening, murmuring that analytic *hmmm* that covers a multitude of responses, asking questions, she interpreted my fears and wishes as I brought them to consciousness. From the beginning she seemed to see through my false composure, my self-protection, to something deep inside me.

For me, the first risk of analysis was to entrust myself to her. Could she hear me? Could I allow myself to be heard? I remember a central moment toward the end of the first year when I began to believe that the answers might be yes. Once, after a particularly difficult session, she bent toward me. "You think no one can—not just know—but truly appreciate, truly feel, the depth of your sadness," she said softly, right by my ear. And, of course, that was true. She had found my secret hiding place, the place where I tried to remain invisible. I lay there rigidly. "What if I can?" she whispered. "That would mean we're very connected." The recognition took my breath away.

Of course, I fought with her: I couldn't bear to believe we were that connected, couldn't bear to need her that much because if I needed her that much I could lose her and how could I stand that? I had this thing I used to do when we got too close, somehow unconsciously disconnect from her, just go away inside myself somewhere; it got to where I could feel myself do it, just pull the plug. It made her feel dead, she said, anesthetized, utterly useless. That made me feel terrible: how could I do that to this person I loved? Maybe it was an unconscious demonstration, she said, my way of showing her what it had felt like to be superfluous, to be the child of an intrusive, narcissistic mother, a woman full of despair who insisted we be one mind, one body.

But even as we struggled, there was pleasure in the exchange, the discovery, the method itself, a pleasure that psychoanalytic theorists (and patients!) seem curiously reluctant to acknowledge, as if to acknowledge it would somehow, in some puritanical scheme of things, lessen the importance of the psychoanalytic project. As another British analyst, Christopher Bollas, ironically observes, "After all, how can this pleasure be justified? Better to emphasize the abstinence, the frustration, the pain, the travails, the pathologies, the resistances, the negative transferences, than to reveal the pleasure that is the source, the aim, and the gratified object of psychoanalysis."

And free association, dream work, and the shared intimacy of the moment are indeed pleasurable. Once, in anguish, I was lying on the couch, experiencing and describing an unpleasant feeling of being tightly bound, wrapped up "like a mummy in a case." I stopped, lay there in silence. Then, from inside that pain, it hit me. "Mummy," I almost shouted, "Mommy, Mother." I was feeling bound and constrained by my relationship to my dead mother and by the way I perpetuated it in my relationship with Dr. Cole. We both began to laugh; it seems obvious now, but it wasn't then, and it was not just the realization but the mind's sheer inventiveness that was a source of deep delight.

We went over that ground like that again and again, and little by little some things began to change. I began at some point to write again, fifteen or sixteen poems over a three-month period, poems that were, I felt, more emotionally honest, poems that seemed to be trying, inch by inch, word by word, to experiment, to go places I'd never gone. Poems that weren't so neat, so controlled, that didn't have good manners and clean faces and every wayward strand of hair caught up in a barrette. Gradually, I began to believe I had a right to my own desires and I was finally able to leave a lover with whom a breakup had seemed necessary for some time. I didn't feel desperate to be in a relationship. I stopped disconnecting so often and then I stopped doing it at all. Well, hardly at all. I no longer felt either an emptiness in my chest or a rock. Sometimes I even treated Dr. Cole like a real person, experienced her as a separate person with her own feelings and desires instead of a figure in the transference.

It's hard to say exactly how or why change happens in analysis. It isn't just that I had bone-deep, shattering insights, though of course I did, moments when the veil was lifted and I felt as if I'd lived a lifetime in forty-five minutes. But knowing isn't enough, especially for someone like me for whom knowing—intellectual understanding—had become defensive knowingness, a defense against feeling. Many contemporary psychoanalysts believe that the change comes about not so much through insight, but through the actual interaction between patient and analyst. Thomas Ogden, for example, talks about the analytic third, an analytic subject created jointly by analyst and analysand, an altogether new being. Chirstopher Bollas writes of the complex ways in which patient and analyst communicate unconsciously, at the level of self to self, a profound kind of knowing and being known. And most would probably agree with Stephen Mitchell that "What the patient needs is not clarification or insight so much as a sustained experience of being seen, personally engaged, and, basically, valued and cared about." That's certainly what it felt like to me. I felt loved.

And then, of course, there comes the time when the patient is ready to leave. When *I* was ready to leave. Or needed to.

I don't know exactly how I knew I was almost ready to terminate, I just did. Part of the change that had taken place in me involved knowing what I felt, being able to trust my instincts. I think I brought it up first, and she agreed that, yes, we were nearly there. We set a date about six months away.

Why leave at all, apart from time and money, not inconsiderable reasons? I don't think there's any one answer, just a number of possible ones. In part because analysis can seem like a suspension of real life, of choice and responsibility, and you intuitively know it's time to take that responsibility for yourself. "Ending is necessary," Mitchell says, "if the analytic work is not to become a static alternative to a fully lived life." But, of course, as Dr. Cole once pointed out to me, "We could always have more to say to each other." There's no such thing as a "complete" analysis.

In leaving, in grieving this loss, she suggested, I would grieve all my losses. It was, of course, what I needed to do. I had always been afraid that if I really grieved, if I really felt my losses deeply—if, for example, I truly mourned my mother's death, truly separated from her—I'd drown in grief, and it had taken two years of analysis before I had allowed myself to cry in an analytic session. It seemed to me that I needed to know, truly know through experience, that I could survive grief in order to fully accept my own authority.

Those last few months were difficult. Like an adolescent about to go off to college, I had mixed feelings: I wanted to go and I was scared to go. I knew that Dr. Cole and I would always be connected by what we had shared, that she would always be an important part of my life, that I could come back to see her when I wanted to—sometimes I envisioned her as a tiny little redheaded figure inside me—but in the course of analysis, I'd come to experience the knowledge that people aren't interchangeable, and I grieved for the loss of *her*. The specific person.

Also, of course, I didn't want to give up this "parent," this person who had in a sense taken care of me. Once she asked me what I felt like doing and I said I wanted to chain myself to her chair. Sometimes when I regressed like that it seemed as though we had to go through the whole analysis in condensed form all over again. It began to seem as though my fingers were stuck on the buttons of a VCR: *Fast forward. Rewind. Fast forward. Rewind. Fast forward.* But, almost despite myself, changes took place, solidified.

At a friend's fiftieth birthday party, the favors were cardboard tiaras, and the next day I thought to take my tiara to analysis because Dr. Cole could use it in the box of toys she kept for her child patients. At least that's why I thought I was taking it. Once, during a session, I had had a vision of myself, a kind of waking dream, as a baby wearing a crown, and I came to refer to my infantile self, the one that wants to be omnipotent (and believes she is), as "the baby with the crown" or "the little princess." While I was sitting in the waiting room that day, it suddenly occurred to me to put the tiara on my head. When Dr. Cole opened the door and saw me, she broke into laughter.

"Should I be forewarned?" she asked, as I followed her down the hall to the consulting room.

"No," I said, "I think I want to leave this with the real babies. I don't need it anymore." I put the tiara in the middle of the little blue table in the children's playroom. I hadn't known I was going to do that, but it seemed immensely important to me, a symbolic act that indicated I was, perhaps, at last growing up. I was fifty-one.

Sometimes my dreams, like the dream of the tornado in the carpet, brought me hard-won knowledge, showed me how far I'd come. And often this was painful, but there was a kind of pleasure in it, too, the pleasure of giving up illusions, of facing things clear-eyed, straight on, and a pleasure in the playfulness, the surprising inventiveness of the dreams themselves. In one, I wandered a universe devastated by some kind of plague; there were moments of kindness among people in the dream, but I had a sudden, searing revelation that I was alone and that that was to be my fate. It was a revelation, I believe, of the human condition, a given for each of us. In another dream from those last days of analysis, my mother turned into Bugs Bunny, who turned into a dead Viking princess whose body was floated out to sea on a coffin ship. Finally, the "princess" metamorphosized into Death itself, complete with shroud and scythe and looking something like the wailing figure in Edvard Munch's painting "The Scream," and at that point in the dream I laughed and called out, somewhat triumphantly, "You can't fool death!" Through a complex chain of associations, I came to believe that my unconscious was both allowing me to face the inevitability of death, of loss, and, in a sense, to "bury" my mother and to let go of her feelings of fear and despair which I had incorporated as my own and which kept me from living my own life to its fullest.

One day, of course, I simply (simply!) walked out of Dr. Cole's office, in tears, and did not go back the next day or the next week or the next month. And did not drown.

Once I had believed that in psychoanalysis I would find a magic cure, all problems solved, all impulses mastered, all things revealed. That I would be rescued, saved, that things would be easy. It's a notion of progress that we Americans, with our self-help books and our Prozac and Paxel and our short-term therapies, find hard to give up; we're still the Puritans looking for "the city on the hill," the promised land. The shortcut to salvation. (As my friend the novelist Allan Gurganus once said, the perfect title for the Great American Novel would be *Self-Improvement*.)

But psychoanalysis doesn't work quite that way. Instead, one day a month or so after the end of analysis, I was visiting a friend's cabin in the Texas hill country near Austin, sitting in the cold, shallow water of a narrow river overhung with huge live oaks, and I looked up at the light leafing through the branches and I suddenly realized I felt something inside me, an actual entity, like an organ, that I'd never felt before. Maybe it's what other people have always felt, but it was new to me. Solid and full. What, for lack of another name, I call the self. And I was shot through with happiness.

Shortly before the end of analysis, I wrote a long poem in eight parts, "Leafing," a poem about the relationship between grief and growth. It is, among other things, a meditation on past and present, connection and separation, the tangos of Astor Piazzola, pecan harvesting in Texas, the rape and murder of a twelve-year-old girl, Wordsworth's "Prelude," *The Scarlet Letter,* and Schubert's *Quintet in C Major*. Without ever referring directly to psychoanalysis, the poem attempts to reproduce the feelings one feels in the course of a psychoanalysis, from despair to joy, from sadness to reasonable contentment, though not necessarily in a straight line. It is ultimately, I think, a celebration of the work Dr. Cole and I did together; even the title, "Leafing," echoes her name, "Letha," though I wasn't conscious of that when I chose it. The poem also tries to reproduce something of the shape of psychoanalysis, which I have come to think of as a spiral: you work through experiences and feelings again and again, each time, perhaps, at a deeper level. The process, I believe, will last a lifetime. Maybe that, too, is the meaning of the tornado in the carpet, what I was seeing in my dream. And, of course, though this may be begging the question a bit, the spiral is also the shape of life itself: of the Milky Way, or galaxy, and, in double form, of DNA, the basic element of life.

Later, I wondered if the dream I came to think of as "The Tornado in the Carpet" was unconsciously related to the short story by Henry James called "The Figure in the Carpet," a story that I had read in graduate school and "forgotten." In it, a famous writer, Hugh Vereker, tells the narrator that no reader has ever discovered the secret message of his writing, "the thread on which all the pearls are strung." It is something, the narrator thinks, "in the primal plan; something like a complex figure in a Persian carpet." The narrator passes this information on to his friend Corvick, a critic, who in turn enlists the help of his fiancée, Gwendolen Erme, who later becomes his wife. The three of them devote years to trying to find out the secret, but by the end of the story all but the narrator are dead and the secret remains unknown. Some have interpreted the story as being about the interrelationship between reader and writer, or about the act of reading itself, or about the writer's inability to control what the reader sees in a work of art. I've wondered whether there was ever really a secret in the first place, to what extent James's story is about the futility of looking for what's not there and thus missing the pleasure of what is.

By its very definition, the unconscious is unknowable, and so it follows that a person must in some sense remain essentially unknowable to herself. Perhaps, Adam Phillips suggests, instead of searching for "wholeness" we should be searching for ways to bear our strangeness. ("Tragedy is when we are ruined by our insufficiency, comedy is when we can relish it.") Though symptoms may sometimes be cured, Phillips says, "there is no cure for the unconscious, no solution for unconscious desire. Knowledge can't put a stop to that, only death can."

Writing this essay, I suffered from terrible, constant pain in my neck and shoulders, pain that radiates up to my head and down my arms. I'd experienced pain like this before during emotional stress, but not since the end of analysis three months before, and I wondered if it had to do with sitting at the computer for long periods of time or with the stress of being on a deadline. Three times I said to a friend that I had thought I wouldn't have stress-related pain like that after analysis, and each time I said it without any consciousness of the irony of what I was saying, since the essay was in fact about giving up that very notion! The third time I said it, I heard myself: the pain was the pain I was writing, the pain of really acknowledging that analysis was indeed over and that there was indeed no ultimate state of perfection.

Maybe the secret of the tornado in the carpet is just that: that there is no secret, no primal plan, no cure, no state of perfection, no life without conflict and ambivalence. The unconscious believes in us and remains that thing of which we cannot be cured; it remains infinitely surprising, showing us how little we know. What I know is the truth of uncertainty. To believe otherwise is to believe in the myth of the straight line, the myth of progress.

CONTRIBUTORS

PEARL ABRAHAM is the author of the novel *The Romance Reader.* She lives in Manhattan, where she is at work on her second novel.

JOHN BARTH is the author of more than ten novels and several short story collections, as well as books of essays and nonfiction. His novels include *The Sot-Weed Factor, Giles Goat-Boy, Letters, The Tidewater Tales,* and *Once upon a Time. The Floating Opera* and his story collection *Lost in the Funhouse* were finalists for the National Book Award. He is a professor emeritus at Johns Hopkins University and lives in Chestertown, Maryland.

ALAN CHEUSE, book commentator for National Public Radio's *All Things Considered,* produces and hosts *The Sound of Writing,* the NPR syndicated fiction/short story magazine of the air. He is the author of a memoir, *Fall out of Heaven,* a story collection, *The Tennessee Waltz,* and two novels, *The Grandmother's Club* and *The Light Possessed.* He teaches at George Mason University.

NICHOLAS DELBANCO is the author of seventeen books. His novels and story collections include *In the Middle Distance, Sherbrookes, The Writer's Trade, In the Name of Mercy,* and most recently, *Old Scores.* He is cofounder of the Bennington Writing Workshop with the late John Gardner, and is the long-time director of the MFA in writing program at the University of Michigan.

ANNIE DILLARD, winner of the 1975 Pulitzer Prize in nonfiction for *Pilgrim at Tinker Creek,* is the author of a novel, *The Living,* and several books of prose, including *An American Childhood, The Writing Life, Living by Fiction, Holy the Firm,* and *Teaching a Stone to Talk.* Her next book, from which "The Wreck of Time" is taken, will be published in 1999. She lives in Middletown, Connecticut.

BRUCE DUFFY is the author of two novels, *Last Comes the Egg* and *The World As I Found It.* He has written on many subjects for national magazines and is a recipient of a Guggenheim Fellowship, a Whiting Writer's Award and a Lila Wallace–Reader's Digest Award. He lives in Silver Spring, Maryland.

ALAN LIGHTMAN has written for *Granta, Harper's,* the *New Yorker,* and the *New York Review of Books.* His books include *Origins, Ancient Light, Great Ideas in Physics, Time for the Stars, Dance for Two,* and two novels, *Good Benito* and *Einstein's Dreams.* He is Burchard Professor of Science and Writing, and senior lecturer in physics, at the Massachusetts Institute of Technology.

BILL McKIBBEN is the author of *The End of Nature, The Age of Missing Information,* and most recently, *Hope, Human and Wild: True Stories of Living Lightly on the Earth.* A former staff writer for the *New Yorker,* he has written for dozens of national publications, from the *New York Review of Books,* the *Atlantic,* and *Harper's* to *Rolling Stone.* He lives in the Adirondacks.

NOELLE OXENHANDLER writes regularly for the *New Yorker* and other national magazines and literary journals. She lives in Sonoma County, California, where she conducts a private writing workshop.

ISHMAEL REED is the author of more than twenty books—novels, essays, plays, and poetry, including the recent *Airing Dirty Laundry* (nonfiction) and *Japanese by Spring* (novel). He has been nominated for the Pulitzer Prize and has been a finalist for the National Book Award. Cofounder of the Before Columbus Foundation, which promotes multicultural American writing, he teaches at the University of California at Berkeley.

JAMES RESTON, JR., has written ten books, two plays, and numerous articles for national magazines. His books include *Galileo: A Life, Sherman's March and Vietnam,* and *Our Father Who Art in Hell: The Life and Death of the Reverend Jim Jones.* His most recent book is *The Last Apocalypse: Europe in the Year 1000* A.D. He lives in Washington, D.C.

KIRKPATRICK SALE is the author of eight books, including *Dwellers in the Land: The Bioregional Vision, Rebels Against the Future: The Luddites and Their War on the Industrial Revolution—Lessons for the Computer Age, The Green Revolution: The American Environmental Movement,* and *The Conquest of Paradise: Christopher Columbus and the Columbian Legacy.* He lives in New York City.

PORTER SHREVE worked at the *Washington Post* for four years before taking a June Rose Colby Fellowship in the University of Michigan's M. F. A. in creative writing program. He lives in Ann Arbor, where he has completed his first novel, *The Obituary Writer.*

SUSAN RICHARDS SHREVE is the author of ten novels, among them *Miracle Play, A Country of Strangers, The Train Home,* and most recently, *The Visiting Physician.* She is an award-winning children's author, former president of the Pen/Faulkner Award for Fiction, and co-editor of an essay collection, *Skin Deep: Black Women and White Women Write about Race.* She is a professor of English at George Mason University.

JANNA MALAMUD SMITH is a practicing social worker and psychotherapist and author of the recent book *Private Matters: In Defense of the Personal Life.* She has published essays and articles about biography, privacy, and her father, the writer Bernard Malamud. She lives in Milton, Massachusetts.

DEBORAH TANNEN is the author of *You Just Don't Understand: Women and Men in Conversation, Talking from 9 to 5: How Women's and Men's Styles Affect Who Gets Heard, Who Gets Credit, and What Gets Done,* and many other books and articles. University Professor and professor of linguistics at Georgetown University, she has also been the McGraw Distinguished Lecturer at Princeton University. She lives in Washington, D.C.

REBECCA WALKER is a contributing editor to *Ms.* magazine and has written articles for a number of other magazines. She is editor of *To Be Real: Telling the Truth and Changing the Face of Feminism* and co-founder of Third Wave, a multicultural organization which initiates young women's activism. Named by *Time* magazine as one of the fifty future leaders of America, she lectures widely on feminism and women's issues. She lives in Brooklyn.

SHAWN WONG is the author of the novels *Homebase* and, more recently, *American Knees,* and has co-edited and edited several anthologies of Asian American literature, including the landmark books *Aiiieeeee!* and *The Big Aiiieeeee!* His work has been awarded a National Endowment for the Arts creative writing fellowship and numerous other prizes. He teaches at the University of Washington in Seattle.

SUSAN WOOD is a poet and professor of English at Rice University. Her second book of poems, *Campo Santo,* was the 1991 Lamont selection of the Academy of American poets.